Before I Do...I will

By

Nikki Simone

© 2001 by Nikki Simone. All rights reserved.

No part of this book may be reproduced, stored in a retrieval system, or transmitted by any means, electronic, mechanical, photocopying, recording, or otherwise, without written permission from the author.

ISBN: 0-7596-4685-6

This book is printed on acid free paper.

1stBooks - rev. 01/02/02

Unless otherwise noted, Scripture quotations that are marked (NKJV) are taken from the Holy Bible, Woman Thou Art Loosed Edition New King James Version Copyright © 1998 by Thomas Nelson, Inc. New King James Version Copyright © 1979, 1980, 1982 by Thomas Nelson Inc.

Scripture quotations that are marked (NIV) are from the Christian Growth Study Bible, New International Version ®. Copyright © 1997 by the Zondervan Corporation. All Rights Reserved.

Scripture quotations that are marked (KJV) are from the King James Version Holy Bible, ®. Copyright © 1973, 1978, 1984 by International Bible Society.

All Hebrew and Greek references noted are from The New Strong's Complete Dictionary of Bible Words. Copyright 1996 by Thomas Nelson Publishers.

This book is dedicated to Gina Grider, who witnessed its conception when God came down and impregnated my spirit,

Glenn Davis, who diligently encouraged me to "push" through until I could see it coming,

And last but definitely not least, My Lord & Savior, Jesus Christ, who was standing at the other end of the delivery table waiting with loving arms to receive what He birthed inside of me.

THANK YOU THANK YOU THANK YOU...

All Glory be to God, my Lord, Savior and Lover. My Best Friend. The One I am honored to call my Husband. Without You, Lord, nothing in my life would be possible. I thank you for blessing me with the wisdom, knowledge, and strength to be Your wife.

Mom and dad, you two have always said to me "You may not thank me now but you'll thank me later." Now is the time for me to swallow my pride and let you both know that you were right. Thank you for showing me earlier on in my life the importance of a relationship with Christ. You two kept me focused on what mattered the most. I love you guys.

My sister, Ronda, I know it wasn't always easy but thank you for being my sister. You are a special young lady. Whenever I think of you and young women like you, I become more and more grateful that I obeyed the voice of God when He told me to write this book. If you will grasp with all your heart, God's unfailing love, the enemy will never be able to steal away the priceless virtue within you.

Glenn Davis, this book, literally, would not be here if God had not sent you my way. No one has ever believed in me as much as you do. There's no mistake that you are God-sent. THANK YOU!!!

My grandparents, Bishop Milton A. Hobbs and Shirley Hobbs, I wouldn't be where I am today (spiritually or physically) if God had not put you both in my life. I love you much.

My father, Milton B. Hobbs, I thank you for how you always broaden my thinking every time we talk.

My aunt, Pastor Yvette Anderson, you were one of the first women who taught me how to be a lady. You taught me how to tie my shoes at age four and how to drive a car when I was seventeen. By your example, I even learned how to be a true woman of God. Thank you.

My spiritual parents, Pastors Paul & Sharon Dean, I would give you your own separate acknowledgment pages but that still would not express all the gratitude I hold within my heart. I praise God for you both and for the impact you have made on my life and ministry. You set an excellent example for every single (and married) believer at VOG. There aren't many couples in this world that compliment each other as well as you two. Your uncompromising righteousness and undying love for one another minister strength to my spirit. I look at you and I am always encouraged to wait patiently on the Lord. You have taught me how to hold out for the "someday". I love you both.

My favorite "aunts", Angela Culver-Dees and Carmen Braxton, you two women of God have blessed my life so much. Thank you both for your words of wisdom and listening ears. It is because of you two that any brother who wants to consider marrying me will have to come correct, <u>Or Else</u>!

Cheryl Davis-Spaulding, I thank you for awakening the creative spirit within me. Thanks also for being a "sister" to me at a time when true sisterly love is often times mistrusted, misunderstood, and taken for granted. You have an anointed way of proving that this kind of love still exists.

My "roomie" Gina Grider, girl what can I say? (Finally, it's here!) Thank you for sharing a "creative day" with me. Who would have thought it would come this far?

My girl Stephanie Knight, these acknowledgments should extend way beyond this book. You are such a blessing to me (whether you want to be or not). Thank you for all your "constructive" criticism. I've always heard I am my own hardest critic, but I think we are running neck-and-neck. Nonetheless, you are greatly appreciated. Out of all of the people God could have sent my way, I am so glad He sent you.

Christopher J. White III, I thank you for blessing me with your support and for allowing the Holy Spirit to use you in such powerful ways to inspire me. You'll never know how much you truly bless my spirit.

Theresa Green, "Momma", I thank you for being my example of a true worshipper and also for all the support you give in so many ways.

Cassandra Exantus, I thank you for all the girl-to-girl talks. For every "Word from the Lord" that I had for you, you always had one right back for me. I can't express how much you bless me.

Kimberly Mills, I thank you for all of your "word of the day" e-mails and for being a true bestfriend through the years.

Matthew Abalos, "muchas gracias" my Latino brother. I thank you from the bottom of *mi corazon* for taking the time out to bless me with your God-given talents. You remind me of the servant in the bible who was a steward over the talents given to him by his master. Don't hide them. Continue to give and much more will be given back to you.

Hasani Pettiford, you have helped me in so many ways, I don't know where to begin. I can't thank you enough for paving the way for me. No matter how busy you are, you always have time to help a sister out. I thank you for rising above mediocrity to live your dream. Because of brothers like you, I am highly encouraged to live my dream. "Success" is truly in your hands.

Mrs. Shirley Pettiford, I thank you for taking the time out of your busy schedule to be a blessing to me. You barely knew me and yet you invested your time into this book as if I was your own daughter. THANK YOU! May the blessings of the Lord overtake you always.

Shirley Green of Cape May, thank you for your encouraging "testimony" of inner strength, courage, and taking over your town.

To my family, friends, and Visions of God Family Worship Church, thank you for all your love, prayers, and support.

To the reader of this book, thank you for obeying the Holy Spirit by picking up and reading this book. I pray that you will be blessed and encouraged and that you will embrace all God has to offer you with open arms.

Before I do...I Will

Dear Lord,
I know I said it before but I have to say it again
You've been much more than my Savior
You've been way more than a friend

When I'm hanging out with my girlfriends
Doing all the sisterly things we do
While they talk and boast of their husbands
I am smiling 'cause I'm thinking of You

And when they begin to complain
I always have to refrain
'cause I can't find a thing wrong with You

When I lie down to sleep at night
Triceps and biceps are not what I find
Instead there are pillows of comfort, sheets of solace
And there lies my peace of mind

When I open my eyes in the morning
There's no one in the kitchen brewing coffee for me
But what I really need is always waiting
For You don't hesitate to hand me a fresh new cup of mercy

Far better than Sanka
Lord I wanna thank ya
There's not a morning You leave me thirsty

I know that one day I will walk down the aisle
And everyone will be clapping with tears in their eyes and a smile
But in the meantime and in between time I patiently wait
'cause till God sends me a husband He Himself longs to be my mate

He wants to prove He can be our everything
Far more than just the reason why we sing
He desires to be the apple of our eyes
Keep our hearts smiling even when there's no man by our side

And so far He's proven He's all the man I need
Until the day I marry He's my only mate indeed
Before I run to anyone else's arms
I'll let Him show me how love's supposed to feel

That is to say
Lord, I vow to You today
That **Before I do…I will**

-Nikki Simone

Contents

Before I Do… 1

Chapters

…I Will Be The Attractive Single God Is Looking For
    Attention: We've Been Redefined 7
    Who's Playing Hide-N-Go-Seek? 13
    Take Pleasure In Our Position 19

…I Will Break Away From My "Ex" Boyfriend—The Devil
    Now devil, get your S.T.U.F.F. and get out 24
    Give Me My Divorce 32

…I Will Fall In Love Again
    Remaking Love 38
    Love Lessons 42
    Romancing the Stone 52
    God's "Good thing" 59

…I Will Help That Brother Find Me
    He Don't Need Tips, He Needs A Waiter 67
    How'd She Get Her Boaz 72
    Shopping Wisely For What We Want 77
    Have We Met? 87
    Adam's Not Dead, He's Just Resting 92

Finally…I Will 98

Before I Do...

(Please do not skip over this part. It is for the purpose of preparing your heart and mind for what God wishes to say to you through this book.)

There are many single believers today. Each is unique and set apart. Each is fearfully and wonderfully made. Each and every one has a purpose. The purpose that we have goes way beyond finding another single believer to hold in our arms. It goes beyond the wedding bells and a beautifully decorated wedding cake. Some brides-to-be may feel that their purpose begins beyond the veil that is lifted off their faces by an awaiting groom. God desires for us to know that the only place that our true purpose can be found is beyond the veil of His presence. Not only can purpose be found, but also everything we need is in the holy presence of the Lord. It is where our happiness can be found. It is where our strength lies. It is our place of refuge. The presence of the Lord is a place of pleasure.

At a particular time in my life I felt that *my pleasure* was only going to come through a satisfying marriage with someone who knew how to love me. Then I let God take full control of my life, my will, and my heart. After He showed me just a few of the benefits He had to offer me I became convinced within myself that I couldn't have been more correct about what I felt. *I have truly found that pleasure.* The divine pleasure I was looking for came through a satisfying marriage with the <u>only</u> One who knows how to love me like no one else can, Jesus Christ. This type of pleasure can only come from dwelling in "holy matrimony" with the Lord. His love is the kind of love that leaves no contenders. His love is what everyone needs before (and after) they walk down the aisle with anyone else.

There are many books written today telling us what we can and cannot do as single believers. Some of those books explicate with ease the issues that arise in the lives of single believers, yet they neglect to inform us that the God who loves us wants our hands in marriage. He wants a chance to be our mate before anyone else. He desires to prove that He can be all things to us, as well as a husband. *Is it possible for us to be married to the Lord?*

"For your Maker is your husband, the Lord of hosts is His name..." **Isaiah 54:5** (NKJV)

If God can be our everything, can't He also be the *husband* that many single believers long for?

The fact of the matter is that He wants every single believer to know that He can be a mate to us. Our season of singleness should be a season of satisfaction in the Lord. If this is the case then why are there so many unhappy singles? Why is singleness looked upon as being a curse instead of a blessing? That is because some don't take into consideration that being single in the flesh is being spiritually married to Christ. It is being wrapped up in His loving arms each day with no interruptions. We have a perfect opportunity to "taste and see" the goodness of His love. God's love is so good that it can fill whatever voids we have in our hearts. It can make us forget any lack that we feel in our lives. Whenever there is a void in us that goes unfulfilled it is because we have not yet learned how to tap into this love. A believer's season of singleness should be one of the best seasons in his/her walk with

Before I Do...I will

Christ. Not only is this a season to enjoy God's love but this is a time for Him to take pleasure in us as He prepares us to love someone else. This season is not a curse but a course that can teach us how to be wives to the mates God has for us. He wants to present us to our mates like He presented Eve to Adam but first he needs to spend time with us to make us what we need to be in Him.

My purpose through this book is to get you to understand just how beneficial this season is for us. Many believers have made the mistake of being so quick to rush into marriage that they forgot to be single. They focused so hard on the big wedding day, the diamond ring, and the proposed life of bliss that they left Christ jilted at the altar of their hearts. He and all His infinite love were left standing at the altar while they went on to "jump the broom" with someone else. What a mistake that can be because when God stands at the altar, He is never alone. As a groom waits at the altar with his groomsmen, our God is standing at the altar with everything we need to prepare us for our future. When we skip down the aisle with someone else too quickly, not only are we skipping over the opportunity to develop perfect intimacy with Christ as singles, but we are also skipping over our preparation time. Many who have skipped over this time are often confused well into their marriage about the purpose God has for them. That true purpose cannot unfold until they have learned to seek Him for it. I'm not saying that once you get married the chances of you finding your intimacy and purpose in Christ are long gone. That would be foolish to say. God longs to be in an intimate relationship with every one of His children whether he/she is married or single. Yet, why wait until we have a husband to begin allowing God to be our husband? Even more importantly, why wait until after we have married someone else for God to start preparing us for him? While we are still single we have a chance not to make the same mistakes that many others have made.

I started to embrace being single when I realized the blessedness in being a wife of the Living God. If God is good to those who do not acknowledge His name, how good can He be to the one He can call His wife?

The bible says *"He who finds a wife finds a good thing and obtains favor from the Lord."* **Proverbs 18:22** (NKJV)

This scripture gives the connotation that the kind of woman being referred to is one who possesses wifely characteristics. She is a *wife* even before she is found. It didn't say he who finds a woman, but rather it *said "He who finds a wife"*. How can a woman be a wife before she is found if she has never been married? **This woman must first be married to the Lord**. When you become the Lord's wife, it is then that he can teach you how to be someone else's wife. The reason why a man will obtain "favor from the Lord" is because when he finds the wife of God he has truly found a "good thing". She is what God holds priceless in His heart. This woman is a diamond. She is the apple of God's eye. The woman I am speaking about is not a fictional character. I'm not writing about her just so I can fill up the space on this page. She is <u>any</u> woman who will allow God to make her His own. She is the woman that will say, '*Yes, I will*' when He reaches out His heart to propose to her. He is reaching out with a proposal to her right now. He is calling for every woman, who will tell the Lord, *'I will'*.

Before I Do...I will

That is what this book is about. It is saying to God **'Before I do...I will'**. Before I say *'I do'* at the altar, *I will* walk down the aisle of God's unfailing love. Before *I do* expect the Lord to present me to the husband He has for me, *I will* allow Him to be my husband. He wants to show us what He longs to do in the life of the woman who would dare to give Him her heart before she releases it to any other. It is my desire to show you how to tell the Lord 'I will'. Find out why singles are so attractive to God and how you can make sure you are in the place where He can find you. Let me show you how you can set yourself totally free from any and all soul-ties with your "ex" boyfriend—the devil. Learn how you, too, can be blissfully married, yet single. Then, discover how to help a brother who's looking for a wife find a "good thing" in you.

In reading this book it is for the purpose of understanding how much God wants to be in each of our lives before and after we find ourselves at the altar. God is at the altar to take us all beyond where we have ever imagined to be in Him. May this book be a blessing to all that read it. To every single believer, may it help you to prosperously walk down the aisle of God's heart and into the arms of the mate He has for you. I pray that the blessings of God will embrace and enrich your life.

Please say this prayer with me before going any further:

Dear Lord, I thank you for loving me so much that You would take the time to prove Your love to me. Now I ask You to encourage my heart through this season of singleness. Help me to not make the same mistakes that many have before me. Don't allow me to rush into

Nikki Simone

marrying someone else before I have fully turned my heart over to You. I pray that the purpose You have for me in this season will be fulfilled. As I continue to read this book, I ask You to release me to Your love and arrest me with Your heart. Help me to grasp and understand what it really means to be Your wife. Open up my mind and my spirit to learn and apply whatever Word You have for me in this book. In Jesus' name, I pray. Amen.

...I Will Be The Attractive Single God is Looking For

Attention: We've Been Redefined

I once had a conversation years ago with a younger cousin of mine. She was about six years old at the time when she asked me how old I was. I told her my age and was curious when she wrinkled up her nose with a frown. I think I was only twenty years old at that time and I couldn't understand why my age would make her react as such.
"Twenty," she exclaimed. "You're twenty?" Needless to say I was baffled at this point.
"Yes I am," I answered her back.
"And you're not married yet?" were the next few words out of her mouth. I cracked up with laughter at her question yet I realized that she was not kidding at all.
"Well...no," I paused as I pondered on the question.
"Well, what's wrong with you? Don't you want to get married? Doesn't anybody like you?"

I almost wanted to hide underneath the coffee table after she got finished with me. As serious as she was, if I didn't know any better, I might have thought that there was something wrong with me. When I told my family and friends about the conversation they responded, "how cute". Now looking back at this I wonder why being single means wearing a nobody-wants-me sign. It's bad enough that some grown ups think this way but here we had a girl who hadn't even reached puberty thinking like this. Why does being single have such a bad rep? What's the big deal about being single and why are some unhappy being this way?

As I thought on these questions one day, God began to answer me by reminding me that Christianity is also an area that is looked down upon by some. Since its inception, Christianity has been despised, misunderstood, and rejected. Yet, despite the way it is viewed and treated, true believers don't stray from its foundation. Why is this? It is because they understand what it means to be in Christ and the benefits thereof. In order for us to appreciate being single, we must have an understanding of what it means and begin to embrace the benefits that come along with this season.

The first thing to understand is that one of Satan's tactics against believers is having the opportunity to define us before we realize who we are. The very definition of the word "define" means to set the limits of. If we allow Satan to define us, or set our limits, he will have full control of where we can go. He then becomes the author of our fate. When the devil defines *single* he comes up with words like desolate, lonely, frustrated, incomplete, and rejected. When I looked at God's definition of being single, then took a second look at how it is defined by the enemy's standards, it didn't match up at all. Whenever something contradicts what God has spoken it can only be the works of the enemy. One might ask, *Why would he want to change the definition of a single believer?* That is because if we will begin to grasp and live in accordance with God's definition, of who we are, there are no limits to where Christ can take us. Our journeys become hindered or road blocked when we allow our views about who we are to become separate and apart from God's. Our views of who we are and what we stand for can be a stepping stone or stumbling block for the adversary. So, likewise, Satan works tirelessly and strategically towards redefining every believer.

Before I Do...I will

It is no secret that our enemy is trying to define us. He has tried to set the standards of who and what a single believer should be since the beginning of time. He wastes no time at all when he's after our purpose. He starts as young as my six-year old cousin trying to make it seem as though being single is a curse from the Lord. He has sent many events in our lives to try and make us feel rejected, unwanted, and useless. He sends a cold chill across our shoulders while we're lying in our beds at night to remind us there is no one there to keep us warm. He makes sure no one is around to carry out that old dusty and heavy piece of furniture we've been breaking our backs to throw out on garbage day. When we go to the mall, he sends our way every couple in America holding hands and cuddling. As though that is not enough, he bombards the billboards, television, and magazines with happy-looking "superficial" couples ranting on about how blissfully content they are. Even if we are content in our season of singleness, if we are not careful, we can become depressed or frustrated over such schemes. Yet if we are watchful we will see that there is a lot to be learned from observing our enemy.

If we pay close attention to some of the singles out in the world, they look as though they are having the time of their lives. According to them, they are. If we were to ask some of the ones who are truly content about being single why they are not married they will probably tell us *"There's no need to rush"*. *"I'm in the prime of my life"*. *"I'm just taking things slow"*. Why does Satan make it a point to have them stand upon these views while he has some single believers singing *"Nobody knows the trouble I've seen"?* Let us look into Webster's New World Thesaurus definition of the word *single* and then to God's definition.

Nikki Simone

In the thesaurus some of the meanings for single are unique, original, and exceptional. This is a big difference from what the enemy wants us to think. In the eyes of the Father we are each unique, original, and exceptional as well. He carefully crafted each of us. David blessed the Lord when he reflected on how he was "fearfully and wonderfully made." (Psalm 139:14) (NKJV) Before He laid the foundations of the world, He knew us and knew exactly who we would become. He knew how He wanted to direct our lives, who we would marry, and if we would get married at all. No matter the length of time of our singleness, the bottom line is that we were all created single beings. God did not skip over this season of our lives. *Neither should we.*

Just like the singles of the world, this time should be the prime of our lives. Instead some believers feel it's a curse. That is because they don't understand God's definition. Being single does not mean not having a man to go to the movies with on a Friday night. God's intended definitions for His single believers are unique, set apart, complete, and whole. Some think that by getting married that is the way they will become whole. Just because a spouse is often referred to as "the other half" doesn't mean he/she will make you whole. Marriage was never meant to create you or make you a whole person, that is the Lord's job. Rather, marriage is to compliment who you were already made to be. Eve didn't make Adam who he was, she was a compliment to him.

Being single is about being *whole* or the Hebrew word chayah. Chayah means to live or to revive. If we are truly living prosperously as single believers our spiritual lives should be full of vitality. One of the key definitions of vitality is the power to survive. It is no wonder the enemy doesn't want us to be content and whole. He knows that a whole believer is a survivor. Whole believers are more than conquerors in Christ Jesus. There is nothing that the devil can throw their way that can take the life out of them. (Romans 8:35-37) Kaliyl is the Hebrew word for *whole* meaning a sacrifice entirely consumed. When we allow God to make us whole, we become a sacrifice to Him that He can totally consume. God is not looking for a partial sacrifice. He is the "All-Consuming Fire" looking for a sacrifice that is acceptable in His sight.

"I beseech you therefore, brethren, by the mercies of God, that you present your bodies a living sacrifice, holy, acceptable unto God, which is your reasonable service." **Romans 12:1** (NKJV)

A believer is supposed to be an acceptable sacrifice unto God, a sweet smelling savor in His nostrils.

2Co 2:15 says, *"For we are unto God a sweet savour of Christ..."*(KJV)

During my research I also came across the Greek word for *singleness* which is the word aphelotes. This word is connected to another word, phellos. The context of these words is in the sense of a stone stubbing one's foot. In other words, a piece of a rock that pierces, alters, or abolishes one's foot. When I looked further into the word "foot", I came across the definition of trampling or oppression. It excited me to put this all together because it gave me a whole new outlook on what being a single believer is all about. Christ is the Rock. We are all pieces of the Rock (the stones). Our enemy is the trampling or the oppression (the foot) that tries to interfere with the growth of God's kingdom. We have the power to pierce, alter, and abolish this foot or oppression. Have you ever seen a trail of ants working diligently on the ground then you put your foot down in front of them to stop them? That's what the enemy tries to do to take us off course from doing the work of the kingdom. However, if we are truly operating in our singleness as God would desire us to, not only will he not be able to take us off course but he'll be a lot more hesitant about putting his foot down anywhere near us. The devil knows what we have the power to do to this *foot*. He doesn't have to trample over us nor do we ever have to be oppressed by him. In fact, he should be under our feet.

This is sure not Satan's definition of who single believers are. I immediately pictured a cartoon during my research. I imagined us being like small stones or pebbles on the floor and when the enemy rushes our way to try and overpower us we cause him to stumble and fall. There is so much we can do to pierce, alter, and abolish the schemes of the enemy. There are attacks and plans of his that are hindered everyday because of the prayers and praise of the righteous. If Satan can keep us so consumed with loneliness, self-pity, discouragement or being distracted because we have no mates he'll get us to miss the purpose of our singleness. He especially accomplishes this if we are not careful in our interaction with one another. If he can get us to focus too much on one another out of God's proper timing, he can steal away our singleness.

God is attracted to the single believer. He adores us. That is why He goes out of His way to make sure that we know how much He wants to spend time with us. It is no wonder why we are so special to Him. Look at who He created us to be. Our purpose as single believers is to be

Before I Do...I will

Christians full of life. Our lifestyle should be a sacrificial offering unto the Lord that will be pleasing for Him to consume. We are the stumbling blocks to the devil. We should never get so caught up with the idea of marriage that we forget to be single. Remember that this is one of the most important seasons in our walk with Christ. Why rush into eating the "marriage cake" if we have skipped over the main ingredients. There will be no substance there to truly satisfy us. Don't skip over the main ingredient to becoming a satisfied godly wife. That ingredient involves being a satisfied single believer. Satisfied believers know who God has called them to be and they are willing to stand their ground until God calls them to another place.

The devil has already tried to define us, now God wants to redefine us. It is up to us to decide to whom we will give that privilege. Remember that only the Creator can truly define what he has intended for his creation to become. I have decided that I am going where Christ wants to take me. There are no limits to where I can go in Him. Besides that, this season of my life is too important for me to miss. I'm not going to allow the enemy to set my limits any longer. I am who my Creator has chosen me to be. Who are you going to let define you?

Who's Playing Hide-N-Go-Seek?

Remember when we were kids; we enjoyed riding our bicycles through the park until sun down, roller-skating up and down the street, playing "mom" to our adorable little dolls. All these things were fun, yet the game that sticks out in my mind is the all time favorite, Hide-N-Go-Seek. This game was just about everybody's favorite and can still be seen being played by amused children generation after generation. In fact, this game might also be seen being played by many believers today. The only difference is that these believers I am referring to have been playing this game with the Lord. I have just spoken to you in depth about who we are as single believers. Let me now take the time out to share with you how to make sure you are in the right place to receive all that God has for you in this season.

Not being in the proper place that God is calling us to be (whether spiritually, emotionally, or even physically) is what I refer to as playing spiritual Hide-N-Go-Seek. This is when we run off into a place where we would expect God to come and find us instead of going where He wants us to go. This can be extremely detrimental in our walk with Christ because when we play Hide-N-Go-Seek with God, we can miss out on all He has for us, not only in this season but also in seasons to come.

Many single believers still play games of Hide-N-Go-Seek, especially when it comes to the issue of finding a mate. I've seen many times when single believers have gotten distracted in this season. Such distraction caused these believers to come away from the place where God was calling them to abide. They allowed themselves to drift off into a place outside of where God desired them. Whenever we don't stay in a place where He has free reign to control our lives and fill the deep and empty voids in us, we are simply running off to our own place of hiding. Some hide in dating relationships, when, in fact, God called him/her to spend time alone with Him. Some hide in their own self-will, when God called him/her to delight himself/herself in Him. Some have even left a church, job, or residence that God told him/her to remain in. There are many more examples of running to a hiding place. Yet, just

Before I Do...I will

like when we played this childhood game on our neighborhood streets, there comes a time when everyone must come out from hiding.

Many single believers that God has a mate for have questioned why they are single and how long they will have to remain single. Yet, they don't take into consideration that though God does want to bless them, they must first come to the place He has called them to be. When I talk about this particular place God is calling us to abide in, I am talking about the place of obedience. That is the place where He wants us to perpetually dwell in. That place may encompass our ministries, our relationships, and our walk with Christ, etc. If we are not in that place of obedience, we are sure to miss our blessings at the time that God wants to give them to us. I used to ask God, *Is it really possible to miss our blessings? Don't You reserve them until we are ready to come and get them?* God answered me by taking me to the story in Genesis about Esau and how he missed his blessings by not being in the right place. (Gen. 27:30-35) His blessings went to his younger brother Jacob. There was nothing he could do or say to get them back. Think about, for a moment, a UPS package. When a delivery man comes to a house, he knocks. If no one is there to answer the door, he leaves. It doesn't even matter if that person was in close proximity. They were not where they needed to be to receive the package. Very seldom will the UPS man leave a package when no one is home. He needs a signature. When we obey God we sign our signature authorizing Him to bless us. When we do not obey there is no guarantee that the blessing will belong to us.

Perhaps someone reading this has been frustrated about being single. Maybe you've been trying to figure out when it will be your turn to be blessed with a mate.

When I came to a state of frustration in my season of singleness, I asked the Lord, almost in tears, *Where are they Lord? Where are all the good, single men of God?* It was not that men were hard to find in the church but they were either already taken, a relative of mine, or, let's just say, they needed to go lay prostrate at the altar just a few HUNDRED more times before I could even consider looking at them. It seemed as though these men I was inquiring about were no where to be found. I wanted to scream at the top of my lungs, *What are they hiding for*? I asked that question of the Lord one day and to my surprise he had a question for me. **Who's really playing Hide-N-Go-Seek?** *What do you mean Lord?* I thought I had stopped playing that game years ago. That is when God let me know that many still play this game today. The Lord is not in the business of hiding anything from His children.

"...No good thing will He withhold from those who walk uprightly." **Psalm 84:11** (NKJV)

God let me know that many people in their search for the *right one* overlook the *only One* that can bless them. When that happens, it is not that what God has for them is hiding, the problem is that when He reaches out to give them their blessing they are not in the place they need to be to receive it. Hide-N-Go-Seek is fun and amusing when you are a kid, but when you are an adult, if you want to receive the things that God has for you, you must take on the attitude that Paul had when he wrote in **1Cor. 13:11**:

"When I was a child, I spoke as a child, I understood as a child, I thought as a child; but when I became a man, I put away childish things." (NKJV)

If you are still playing this game, it is time to "put away childish things" in order to receive what is due to you.

I can remember the cries of frustration from my younger sister, as we were growing up, who often protested how it was not fair that I got more privileges than she did. My mother quickly, but patiently, pointed out to her that there was an age difference that warranted me the right to receive some of the things that she was not yet allowed to acquire. There were things that we both received simply because we were from the same parents but when it came to some special privileges, it went to the oldest. What I'm saying is that there are some things that God only blesses us with after we've grown up a bit. We have to put away childish things and do away with them for good. Then we will be ready to come to the place God is calling us to.

Hide-N-Go-Seek goes back farther than the games we played in the parks and playgrounds as children. Many men and women in the bible have played this same game in their relationships with God. We can find the first account of it being played in **Genesis 3:8**:

*"...and Adam and his wife **hid** themselves from the presence of the Lord God among the trees of the garden."* (NKJV)

Adam and his wife, Eve, hid themselves in the very garden that God placed them in. Many believers hide today in the purpose where God has placed them. They run behind the trees and bushes of their own will and desires.

God still has to ask the same question that He asked of Adam in the garden of Eden, *Where Art Thou*? Before we take any steps towards the place God has for us in our future we need to find out where we are today. Are we in a place where He can take us to the next step of finding a mate or are we hiding from Him? If we do not allow God to control our lives there is no way He can take us from season to season. That is the problem that many believers who have gotten married out of the will of God seem to overlook. If God didn't bring them into the season they are now in then where are they to go from there? Only God can call them back to where they belong and begin leading them again. We have to be mindful to allow the Lord to lead us <u>at all times</u>. It is not difficult at all to lose our direction. Many have run off to places where they didn't belong and did not realize it until they found themselves being reeled back into God's arms of love. This will not happen if we make the Lord our focus. When we keep our focus on Christ He can lead us wherever He needs us to go. Single believers should always have their focus on God. He is the center of our very existence.

When it comes down to waiting for the blessings that the Lord has in store for us, the only hiding place that is safe to hide in is in the Lord. During the game of Hide-N-Go-Seek, whoever was seeking would count up to ten or twenty and then they would loudly say, *"Ready or not, here I come."* If anyone didn't find a hiding place at that point, they hastily made it to the closest and most inconspicuous place they could find. Jesus is the closest place for us to rest in when we are waiting for our mates.

"...in the secret of his tabernacle shall he hide me; he shall set me up upon a rock." **Psalm 27:5** (KJV)

Before I Do...I will

Christ should be our hiding place. We don't have to bother trying to find one of our own. Come out from your hiding place to receive all God has in store for you. How do you come out from hiding? By being obedient to what the Lord wants in your life and taking the position that you are not going to stay apart from God's will. We all need to get into our "place" in Him. He is the solid Rock on which we can stand and all other ground is merely sinking sand. Why hide when in Him we can abide? He's waiting with open arms to embrace us with His love.

Take Pleasure In Our Position

As single believers it is imperative that we understand God's desire for us is to take pleasure in Him during this season. There are too many people who feel that the pleasure comes after the mate, but that is not so. That is not how God intended it to be. Rather God's intentions were for us to take pleasure in Him as He in return takes His pleasure in us.

"Delight yourself also in the LORD; and he shall give you the desires of your heart." **Psalm 37:4** (NKJV)

We are to delight ourselves in Him. Yet, it is impossible for us to begin to delight ourselves in God if we have not learned to be content in this season.

I used to feel that often times God was being facetious because it seemed the ones who were happy being single ended up getting married the quickest. One would think that God would rush to the needs of the miserable, less satisfied singles and bless them first. However I later came to learn that the single believers who are content are the ones who have learned how to take <u>pleasure</u> in the <u>position</u> that they are in until they have reached the higher level in their <u>purpose.</u> When you take pleasure in your position, your purpose will begin to unfold right before your very eyes.

God gave Adam a position when He placed him in the garden. Adam was to take care of and cultivate the garden he was placed in.

"Therefore the LORD God sent him forth from the garden of Eden, to till the ground from whence he was taken." **Gen. 3:23** (NKJ)

The word Eden, which is the garden in which Adam dwelt, means pleasure. Before God sent Adam a mate he set him in the midst of pleasure and gave him something to do. That is the same way God wishes to deal with us today. God wants our pleasure before we give it to anyone else. The bible says that single women ought to care about the things of the Lord, how she may please Him. (1Cor. 7:32-34). Not only are we to delight in Him, but we should find pleasure in the position where He has placed us. We should take pleasure in serving in our local church, our ministries, etc. Adam took pleasure in his position. He was busy doing what God wanted Him to do. In fact, it was God who looked at Adam and decided that it wasn't good for him to be alone. (Gen. 2:18) The bible does not indicate that Adam mentioned a word about not having a mate. There was no need for him to say anything. When we are busy doing what God wants us to do, He takes care of the rest. If we want to step into our purpose, what we need to do is to begin taking pleasure in what God is telling us to do right now, then we can watch Him go to work on the rest.

Since God desires for single believers to learn how to take pleasure in Him, we shouldn't make the mistake of getting married without first taking pleasure in God. If we do this we may never truly know what our pleasure in this season was intended to feel like. Many people have their own views of how pleasure should feel but if we truly want to be satisfied we have to allow God to show us. How do we become content in God? We become content when we stop worrying about what we don't have and start embracing the One who has always been there—our Lord and Savior. We become content when we have learned to take pleasure in our Lord and in this season. He is not in the business of torturing us or withholding our needs and desires. He does, however, want to make sure that our desires match up with His will. God's will for a single believer is for him/her to learn how to delight in Him.

I urge you to learn to be content. Content singles make content mates. Miserable singles make miserable mates. If you are miserable before you get married, don't think because you get married that you won't continue to be miserable. If you have never learned how to have true pleasure while you are single, then why should you find it when you are married? Pleasure shouldn't be based on how big the engagement ring is or on the firm strong arms of a husband.

If we have not learned how to be happy with someone who has paid the full price for all of our sins, how then do we feel we'll be truly content with someone who just pays the light bill and mows the lawn every other Saturday? All the bills may be paid, food may be on the table, and the gas tank may be filled to the brim, yet there are wives that are still unhappy. I can see a husband flying off the handle and asking, *What does a man have to do, shed blood?* Well, someone already did that, his name is Jesus Christ, and even He finds it difficult to please some of the ones He loves. We shouldn't fool ourselves into believing that we can find true contentment anywhere other than in the Lord. He holds the key to our joy.

One might ask, *so if Adam was so content why would he hide from God?* Adam was content up until he bit into what was forbidden for him to touch. (Gen.3: 6-7) Don't allow the enemy to talk you into biting into the forbidden and unfruitful seeds of discontentment. Discontent believers hide from God. Satan will try his hardest to get us to be unhappy about this season. He'll try to get us to eat spoiled fruit of loneliness, self-pity, or discouragement. Don't give in to the devil. If we take joy in where the Lord has placed us in this season, He will never let us down.

Jeremiah 29:11 says, *"For I know the thoughts that I think toward you, saith the LORD, thoughts of peace, and not of evil, to give you an expected end."* (KJV)

God already has our "expected end" in mind. He already knows what He wants to do through our lives. We have to make the choice to afford Him that opportunity. God has a deeper purpose for us. If we take pleasure in our position, we can't help but to walk into that purpose one day.

Before you move on to the next chapter, take the time to say this prayer with me:

Before I Do...I will

Dear Lord, I thank and praise You for allowing me to see how attractive I am to You. Your definition of who I am is nothing like what the enemy would have me to believe. You think far greater of me than I have ever thought of myself. Thank you for showing me how important it is to be where You want me. I realize that in order for me to receive whatever You have for me, I must let You lead me. Please forgive me for any act of disobedience that I have shown. I repent for any of the hiding places that I have run to that took the place of Your will for me. I now give You full control of my will and I ask You to guide me to wherever You see fit. I trust that You will safely bring me from season to season. I am willing to wait and stand still until Your will is clear to me. I no longer hide from You, but here I am Lord to receive and take pleasure in whatever Your love may have in store for me. Thank you for Your forgiveness, Lord. In Jesus' name. Amen.

Nikki Simone

...I Will Break Away From My "Ex" Boyfriend—The Devil

Now devil, get your S.T.U.F.F. and get out

Satan desires our attention as much as God does. As a matter of fact, the devil doesn't mind very much that we remain "saved", as long as he's got our attention. If he can keep our attention, he has access to our hearts. The devil was a "boyfriend" to us when we were sinners out in the world. When a believer gives his/her heart to the Lord, he/she comes right out of a relationship with the devil. When we become believers, our enemy knows we are making a statement to him that it is over for good. Like any jealous "ex-boyfriend" he doesn't take that loss very well. He will spend whatever time he has left trying to get our hearts back into his arms. He wants to take our hearts away from our Savior. Unfortunately, he has already succeeded with some believers. Their hearts have somehow slipped out of the arms of God and back into the devil's grip. They have become prisoners of war in an ongoing battle for the heart.

How are these soul-ties between the believer and the devil possible? Our hearts can fall back into the enemy's arms if we don't allow God to have full control of our lives, our mind, and our will. Our hearts and souls can become tied up with the enemy's if he can get us to take God out of *first place* in our lives. The devil distracts single believers often times by causing them to focus on putting other people and situations in the place of God. That's when he'll try to get our hearts to drift further and further away from the Lord until it reaches his hands. Some of the symptoms

Before I Do...I will

of having a drifting heart are, feelings of extreme loneliness, constantly reflecting on the past, spending more time dreaming about marriage and your future mate than you do praying and communing with God. If you are experiencing any of these feelings, ask yourself *who are you letting have access to your heart?* Is your heart safe in God's arms or locked within the devil's chambers? We can become imprisoned when we are actually supposed to be "free indeed".

"So if the Son sets you free, you will be free indeed." **John 8:36** (NIV)

That means that once God has set us free from the grip of Satan we don't ever have to be bound by him again.

If you feel that the enemy has succeeded in stealing your heart away by putting it on lock-down and you are looking for the key, I have news for you. If you have allowed God to endow you with His Holy Spirit, you already have it, that key is the power of the Holy Ghost that will enable you to unlock your heart and walk away from the adversary. It may be hard to find this key because of all the other "junk" the devil has been handing you over the years. He does this to fill up your arms and make you forget that you had the key in the first place. Jesus hands it to us after we accept salvation. He took it from the enemy right before His resurrection. In order to find that key we must put down everything that the devil has given us. Christ has made us free but we will still walk around bound until we let loose of the enemy's garbage.

Terry Nance in his book "God's Armorbearer II"[1], explained very well how one could be free—yet bound. He was explaining a television documentary on how Africans capture monkeys. He explained how monkeys are very intelligent. This is why when the Africans put out cages with a trap set on the door and a bright object inside the monkeys were too smart to go in. So the Africans closed the cage and made the wire around the cage just big enough so the monkey could get his hand in the cage. When the monkey saw the bright object, he put his hand through the wire and grabbed it but could not get it out of the cage. With the object in hand, he could not pull it through. He could only be free if he would let go of the object. The devil wants us to keep holding on to "objects". He wants to keep things in our lives so that he can have continual access to our hearts. He knows we will never be free indeed if we don't let go of them.

One of the reasons it was so hard for me to finally break away from an ex-boyfriend was because I kept everything he ever gave me. Everywhere I turned in my house there was something he gave to me. When I finally got fed up I gathered all these things into one big trash bag and said sorry but it's over between us for good. We need to say to the adversary, sorry devil, but it's over between us FOR GOOD! He is truly defeated when we catch on to his schemes and begin to put everything aside to make room for Christ to be first place in our lives again.

We can walk off from Satan's grip into the fresh air of God's holy presence once we put down everything that the Lord didn't give us. God wants us to step into the intimacy of His love, yet we have to first break any and all soul-ties with our ex-boyfriend, the devil. We can't be married to Christ if we allow our "ex" to keep running in and out of our lives. These soul-ties have to be broken for good.

There are two things that have to happen in order for a departing couple to truly go their separate ways. One, they

Before I Do...I will

have to walk away and let themselves out of the relationship. (That's where the key comes in) The other thing that must happen is that somebody has to move out. As long as both are living under the same roof, whatever they say as far as "breaking up" is null and void. Though we can leave the devil, that doesn't mean he is so quick to leave our place. The place I'm talking about now is our lives. Satan often tries to lounge around and wait for us to come back home. When someone is after us as bad as he is they don't give up so easily. That's the misconception that causes a lot of believers to slip back into what they were delivered from. They think he's gone, but not so. They think the coast is clear, they tip back in their place, and securely lock the door behind them. They shut themselves right back up with the devil because they neglected to kick him out. We have to tell the devil to get his "stuff" and get out of our lives. He came, moved into, and got comfortable in the place where we already resided. To make matters worse, he didn't just show up by himself, he brought his "stuff". Just like when someone moves in with another person, they may bring furniture, linen, tools, and their favorite slippers, etc. Well, when Satan comes to move in, he brings the things that make his stay comfortable, which I use as an acronym called S.T.U.F.F. This word represents the Sheets, TV, Utensils, Furniture, and Food that he brings to our domain. Let me break this down.

The *sheets* that he brings into our lives are the sheets from our past that wrap themselves around our waist to bind our lives. At first they may feel warm like they are protecting or comforting us. We may find that we keep them around because our past is apart of our comfort zone. It's what we are familiar with. Yet, these sheets were designed to keep us in situations that we know we should not be wrapped up in. Satan wants to keep us constantly in his bed of confusion, worry, fear, and doubt. He usually uses things from our past to do so. He uses what he already knows about us to bind us. Just like in a literal sense, if we walk around in those sheets long enough, we won't be able to make too many steps without tripping. Walking around with sheets is a dangerous situation. Sheets are something only God can remove. If you have sheets around you, this is the chance to ask Him to remove them. Once He does, don't go jumping back in the bed. Give the devil back his sheets by leaving the past behind.

"Stand fast therefore in the liberty wherewith Christ hath made us free, and be not entangled again with the yoke of bondage." **Gal. 5:1** (KJV)

We can't allow ourselves to be entangled with the devil again.

The next thing that Satan brings is his TV. Now, I'm not a television person. I can go all year without watching one single show. For someone who is, they may agree with me that it's hard to survive without one. Well, it is also hard for our adversary to survive in our lives without the TV that he brings. His TV does not stand for television but rather ***tunnel vision***. When I looked up the words tunnel vision in the Webster's New Complete Medical Dictionary the definition stated that it was a *constriction of the visual field resulting in loss of peripheral vision*. Peripheral vision means the outer part of the field of vision. The devil wants to come and set his *tunnel vision* right in the midst of our lives. He wants to cut our spiritual vision short by constricting our visual fields. In essence, what I'm saying is when we have no peripheral vision we become restricted in what we can see. Satan wants to cause us to not be able

Before I Do...I will

to see beyond what is sitting right in front of us. He'll cause us to get discouraged and give up if we can't see anything but the negative situations he places right in front of our lives. Yet, it is when we can see on the sides of us that no matter what we go through we can bear witness that the Lord is there. **Psalm 124:2** reads:

"If it had not been the Lord who was on our side, when men rose up against us, then they would have swallowed us alive. When their wrath was kindled against us, then the waters would have overwhelmed us, the stream would have gone over our soul; then the swollen waters would have gone over our soul." (NKJV)

David didn't allow the enemy to set up tunnel vision in his life. He had many enemies. He had to constantly look over his shoulder and watch his back. However, he didn't allow his circumstances to restrict him from seeing that the Greater One was always on his side. Have you ever seen someone just stuck in front of the television not able to move? They sit there even through the commercials and everything around them seems to be non-existent. The enemy wants our eyes glued on what he's laying before us so that we can't see the Hope of Glory on our side. We can't allow the enemy to put up tunnel vision in our lives. If we have our spiritual peripheral vision in operation, even if we are forced to look at the situation that is right in front of us, God will show us another way out.

Utensils are the next of the "stuff" the enemy brings to our lives. These are the things that he uses to stir up strife. He uses them to flip over positive things to make them look bad. He tries to pat down our blessings so that we can hardly see them. He tries to drill fear into our minds, hammer down our faith, and drive nails of discouragement through our hearts. Whatever he can use to keep us bound, he will. When we become aware of these devices that he uses, that's when his tools become powerless.

The main thing that Satan brings with him to our place is his *furniture*. These things are what he rests and gets comfortable in. He becomes secure in knowing that piece of furniture, no matter how old it is will hold him up and keep him firmly where he dwells. These pieces of furniture are the truths that the devil uses to make us feel guilty, ashamed, and unworthy. They are the failures, sins, and shortcomings that we encounter with our own flesh constantly. He holds these things over our heads like a lamp post, making sure that we can see our wrong and then tells us that we will never be what God wants us to be so we might as well give up. He can rest safely and comfortably as long as he has something to lie down on that keeps us believing that we have no right to be free from him. When we let these things get the best of us and we don't confess our sins and give them to the Lord, that's when the devil knows he's there to stay.

The last items of the "stuff "he brings is *food*. Satan tries to cook things up in our lives in order that he may keep us in bondage. He'll feed us things telling us we're not worth much. He'll feed to us situations that may cause us to lose faith in God. He wants to keep us full of strife, worry, and doubt. We cannot allow the enemy to feed us these things. Such things can become like salmonella to our spirits. Salmonella is an intestinal bacterium that causes food poisoning and possibly disease. Many Christians today are suffering spiritual food poisoning due to what he/she has allowed the enemy to feed into his/her spirit. This food poisoning causes a spiritual illness within the body of Christ that makes it difficult for the body to function effectively. No wonder when the Word of God is brought forth, in many instances, it is hard for many believers to properly digest it and to become doers of the Word. We cannot let Satan feed us and then try to wash it down with the Word. Don't eat what he brings to you. It could never be for your good.

Regardless of what the devil tries to bring we should be happy to know that we don't have to live with it. In verse 6 of **Psalm 124** David goes on to say:

"Blessed be the Lord who has not given us as prey to their teeth. Our soul has escaped as a bird from the snare of the fowlers. The snare is broken and we have escaped. Our help is in the name of the Lord, who made heaven and earth." (NKJV)

Thank God that our help is in the name of the Lord. How will you tell the devil to get his "stuff" and get out? You'll do it in the name of the Lord. He's an illegal resident and he has absolutely no right to live with us. Jesus took away that right. Don't let the enemy trick you into believing he can stay. The devil is a liar. He's got to go not us. Most of us will not just let any stranger off of the streets come into our homes. Don't allow the devil to stay there either. The longer he stays, the more "stuff" he'll accumulate. As a close friend of mine would say," Tell that joker to get his S.T.U.F.F and get out". Don't let him leave a thing behind. Like in a relationship between two people, if someone leaves something behind it gives him/her a chance to come back. Before you know it, that person will find a way to creep back into his/her lover's life. Don't let the enemy do that. Kick him out of your life for good. Then pray to God that He stays out.

No demon in hell is going to try to run my house while I'm there. Especially when this "temple" was already paid for. That would be like leaving a beautiful home, after it has been fully paid for, because of an invasion of insects. Before anyone would think twice about leaving, they would most likely pay a top exterminator to get rid of the problem first. Satan is a pest when it comes to this temple we dwell in. He tries to get all in the cabinets of our minds, the pantries of our hearts, and the windows of our souls. When we allow the exterminator, Jesus Christ, to move in the place where the enemy once dwelled He will make our house the home it needs to be. Let go of the "ex" so you can move on to the love that is waiting to capture your heart. Christ is waiting to expose you to a love affair that not even a mate can give. Are you ready to drop your "ex" for good and give the Lord a try?

Give Me My Divorce

I am often blessed by the life changing words and testimonies of God's people. Especially when these words "hit home" in my life. When I heard for the first time Prophetess Juanita Bynaum's powerful message, 'No More Sheets', I was astounded by how potent and candid that word came across. She was reflecting on a conversation she once had with God about why she was single. Prophetess Bynaum had already been married at one time in her life but somehow found herself back in the arms of singleness and she questioned God about why she was single again. She went on to say how God told her that the reason she could not get married again was because she was not single. I can imagine how she felt when He told this to her. I know I would have been extremely confused by those words. *Lord, what do you mean I'm not single?* Prophetess Bynaum went on to explain that the reason God said she was not single was because she was spiritually still attached and entangled with her past. She gave an excellent analogy of this entanglement by wrapping various sheets around her waist to show how many believers walk around with the sheets of their past still enveloping them and how only the Lord himself can unwrap these sheets.

This message brought forth many questions in my mind that forced me to give myself a spiritual reality check. I began to ask myself, *How many of the consequences of my past sins was I still wearing? How many stolen hearts did I carry around that did not belong to me? Better yet, where was my own heart and soul, did I still have them or did I give them away somewhere along the line to some stranger I'll never see again?* I could hear a voice clearly asking me, *What are the names of the designer labels on your sheets*? Yes, we may be single physically, but spiritually and emotionally are we still married to someone or something else? Are we still entangled in sheets of our own with the designer labels of our past? If we are, we cannot expect for God to bring us a new love until we rid ourselves of the old. That would be like putting a fresh new comforter on a bed but never changing the sheets. No matter how good that comforter feels, our rest won't feel complete until we get rid of the sheets.

Some women today complain about not being able to find a mate. Yet, they are not spiritually and emotionally single. If we look at these women long enough we will see the bondage over their lives. They don't even look free. There may not be a physical person involved in their lives but spiritually what is binding them won't let them go. The people, places and experiences that have connected with

Nikki Simone

their souls are still holding on. They walk like they have a ball and chain attached to their ankles. All the makeup in the world and the sharpest high-heeled pumps cannot cover up the emptiness that has arrested them. These women aren't single at all. They are involved in a "common law" marriage situation because they have never gotten rid of their sheets by giving them to the Lord.

Some of us may still be walking around like these women. God knows this and He also knows that He cannot allow us to enter into any relationship He has for us until we are totally single again. Nor can God embrace us with the fullness of His unfailing love until we are ready to become free. These sheets must be untied from our lives by the Lord.

How does this "common law" marriage from our past occur? The definition of common law is an unwritten law based on custom, usage, etc. We make our pasts part of our custom or usage when we neglect to leave them behind us. When we don't let God free us from our past, it becomes a comfortable part of our lives. Before we know it, if we allow these things to abide with us for too long it becomes a "common law" for them to stay. However, God's law takes precedence over any other laws. God's law has made us free from bondage.

"For the law of the Spirit of life in Christ Jesus hath made me free from the law of sin and death." **Romans 8:2** (KJV)

We don't have to continue to be married to the sheets of our past.

How does one break totally from this marriage? The only way out of a marriage is through a divorce. There needs to be a divorce from our past. We can't just think we can walk away. We have to allow God to undo or "divorce" us out of these situations. The word divorce means a cutting of the matrimonial bond; to drive out from a possession; to be fully freed or released. When God divorces us from something, He sets us at liberty. We don't have to be bound by these things any longer. Many who are oppressed do not think they are because they can't physically see what has a hold on them. Anything that hinders God from being able to hold us freely in His arms has a hold on us whether physical, emotional, or spiritual. If He sees that we're not "single" in any of these three areas, He's not going to rush to give us a mate. *Why should God give us a mate if we are not single?* He has to first make us complete by tearing off the layers of sheets that have wrapped themselves so tightly around our lives. He wants to free our minds, free our bodies, and free our spirits. While we are waiting for a mate He wants to make sure we're free to receive one.

Go to whatever is binding you and demand a divorce. Demand your freedom from these things by giving them to the Lord through prayer and letting Him release you. Our judge is Jesus and He is on our side. We have no choice but to win if we let Him grant us our divorce. He will do it gladly but we have to really want it. Out of all the many times I broke up the relationships with any of my ex-boyfriends, I can honestly say that I didn't really want a divorce until that very last time when I finally gave the relationships over to God. God is not going to free us unless that is our desire. We have to make a decision about whether or not we want a divorce. If you stay with your past long enough, it will try to rob you of who God blessed you to be. Don't let that happen. Let God do what He has to do today. If you ever want to be happily married you have to become fully divorced.

A divorce can be a battle because even when you walk away, that doesn't mean that who or what you are divorcing yourself from will be as willing to say 'bye-bye'. Yet, nothing is impossible with God. It can be done. God made me a promise that He's making with all of us right now. If we will let go of what isn't ours, He will be free to bless us with what is ours. God's not just going to throw His blessings for us into already filled arms. He'll wait until we lay aside those things. We often times expect God to just rain down His blessings upon us but if we're holding on tight to an umbrella of past relationships and/or situations how then can He soak us with this "rain". We have to put down what is in our embrace. We need arms that are free to receive from Him. God has a blessing with your name on it. Don't miss out. Don't listen to your situations. These situations will lie to you and tell you that you are still indebted to them. Christ has already set us free. Let go and let God caress you with what He has for you.

For anyone that has trouble letting go of the past and getting rid of the devil (for good), say this pray with me:

Lord, You have made it perfectly clear to me that my heart belongs to You. Yet I must admit that it has been difficult for me to keep it placed in Your hands. I know that we should not be entangled with the yoke of bondage yet the enemy is constantly trying to hold me back from Your love. I ask You Lord to help me to release the things that don't belong in my arms. I repent for holding on to things that You did not give to me. I lay those things down by faith right now so that I may pick up what You have for me. **I speak to you, Satan, right now and I say that you have been in my life long enough. Get your S.T.U.F.F. and get out! You are no longer welcome in this place. I also demand, at this very moment, a divorce from my past.** *Lord, I give my past over to You and I ask You to release me from the sheets that have surrounded my life. Thank you Savior for untangling me and taking me back into Your loving arms. Here is my heart. Do with it as You please. I bless You and I declare that I am finally ready for You to show me how to be Your wife. In Jesus' name, I pray. Amen.*

Nikki Simone

...I Will Fall In Love Again

Remaking Love

I remember when I finally made the decision to be totally available to God. I was sick and tired of running in and out of empty and non-gratifying relationships. I had run my "well of love" completely dry as I gave it to all the wrong people. It was Bishop T.D. Jakes who said in his book "The Lady, The Lover, and The Lord,"[2] "There is nothing worse than giving the right thing to the wrong person." He couldn't have been more correct. When you are giving to the wrong person, there is absolutely no guarantee of a return. Everybody needs something in return. Even God is looking for a return of praise and worship from the ones He loves. There is nothing wrong with wanting something in return. In fact, we'd be fooling ourselves if we said we didn't expect a return from anyone. When we love, we expect a return. When we give, we expect a return. The more we give, the more we'd like to receive in return. Let's think about it. It is much easier to tell a cashier to keep the change when he or she just owes us a nickel or a penny. However, if we've handed over a one hundred dollar bill and the item we wanted to purchase only amounted to five or ten dollars we would most likely stay at the cash register and expect every cent that's due us. As a matter of fact, if the cashier doesn't have the adequate change we'd rather put the item back and walk out the store without it then to not receive a return. It's a terrible feeling when we don't receive a return.

The non-satisfying relationships I was involved in never gave me the return of love I needed. I kept giving out until I was left with barely enough love for myself. I decided at that point to finally give the little that I had left to God. When someone has been in and out of dead-end relationships it may seem as though there is hardly anything to conjure up to give. Yet, no matter how little we think we have to give, our Jehovah-Jireh always has a way of making something out of nothing. It is a pity when someone overlooks God and gives the love meant for Him to someone else. That is not to say that a man can't love us, but when we give love to God *first*, He can do more with that love than anyone could ever dream or imagine. He is the Master of multiplication.

When Jesus was faced with a situation of not having enough to feed a multitude of people He took the little that He had to work with. He blessed it, broke it, and gave it to His disciples to feed the multitude. (Mark 6:41-42) The Lord dealt a great deal with me about this particular passage; mainly because He knew the little amount of love I had to give Him was barely enough for myself, let alone for someone else. Yet, He had compassion on me as He did for the multitude of people He fed. When I made a conscious decision to give my love to Him, He didn't just take it and give me nothing in return as in my other relationships. Jesus took it, blessed it, broke it, and gave it back to me. This is what He wants to do with the love of believers today. The Lord's heart is still full of compassion for the multitude. He sees the dry "wells" of love that many carry around with them. He is aware of the dryness they have been experiencing in their hearts. He knows that what they have to give is not enough.

After a spiritual divorce there needs to be a *remaking* of love. Jesus can't just send us away just like He could not send the multitude of four thousand away the day He blessed them. (Matt. 15: 32) His concern was that they were too hungry to be sent away. They needed to be fed so they would not faint along their journey back home. He sees how hungry we are for His love. He cannot send us away, lest we faint in our Christian walks. When the enemy fondles our hearts, he can leave them in pretty bad shape. Jesus was sent to "heal the brokenhearted". (Luke 4:18) He takes our love into His own hands. First, He blesses it. When I was a little girl I remember when I first learned how to bless my food. I referred to it as saying "grace". I was taught there were two reasons why I should say my "grace". The first reason was to give thanks. The second reason was so that God would take out all impurities and make it clean enough to eat. When the Lord blesses our love He takes it in His hands and takes out impurities. He makes it like His own love. He makes it clean enough for Him to partake in. Then He breaks our love. This is when we may feel that our love is being abused. It feels like it is being torn apart. What is really happening is that Jesus is making it ready to give to another. He wants to make what was barely enough for you, more than enough for two. He causes it to multiply.

Many single believers dream about weddings and mates but they have not considered that what they have to give someone else has to be placed in God's hands first. If there is a lack of love within it must be placed into the hands of the Anointing. There are some believers who get married expecting for someone else to fill their areas of lack. A mate cannot "fill up" any place within us that was meant for God. Man can't make your love. Man can only take your love. Yet, if you allow God to remake love in you, your "well" will never run dry.

Before I Do...I will

I used to complain about the love that I was not getting from others instead of paying attention to my own lack within. If Jesus' disciples would have brought forth the bread and fish then tried themselves to distribute the food, there would not have been in any way enough to feed to the multitude. It had to first pass through the hands of the Lord. This is what we try to do when we give our love away without first giving it to Christ. We try to make it enough by ourselves but only He can. Many couples experience failed marriages today because these couples tried to distribute their love to one another without first handing it over to the Lord.

Whatever Jesus gives, He gives it to us to give to another. He didn't cause that bread and fish to multiply just for Him and His disciples but for the multitude as well. God wants to remake our love not only for our future mates but for the future of the multitudes. Not just for our future households but for the body of Christ. There are a lot of believers who fail to possess this more-for-the-multitude mentality. In other words, people want to be blessed for themselves and their households. When they pray to God for blessings it most likely does not extend beyond their immediate surroundings and into the hands of the corporate body of people. Whatever Jesus did it was to bless more than the few standing around to witness it. There are so many examples of how His love extended beyond just those around Him. God wants us to get out of the mindset of the more-for-me blessings and step into the realm of the more-for-the-multitude blessings. By the same token, God wants singles that He can not only prepare for their mates but for the multitude. Marriage was never meant to be the end all to be all. There is work to do for the kingdom before and after marriage. God does not expect us to get married, have a family, and live happily ever after in our little closed-off worlds. With the mate He gives us, we should move on toward kingdom business together.

What if we stopped thinking about marriage for ourselves and started thinking about it for the multitude? What if we grasped the concept that two gathered in the name of Jesus is a powerful force for the Lord? God is searching for single believers He can trust who will give up the love He has given them and allow Him to take, bless, break, and make their love for the multitude. How much more blessed would our marriages be if they were made for the multitude? How much more strength would our marriages exemplify if we not only ministered to our mates, but with our mates we ministered to someone else? This is the type of mindset God is looking for His singles to have. There is nothing wrong with desiring to get married but we must understand that our purpose goes beyond the arms of a spouse. There is a divine destiny waiting. We can't allow it to pass us by. A multitude is awaiting your love. How much do you have to feed them? Whatever the amount, give it over to the hands of Jesus.

Love Lessons

How can we give our love totally over to the Lord? We can do this by handing Him our hearts. We have to let down the walls that have been surrounding our hearts and let Him take pleasure in us. Many find it difficult after a divorce to let down their guards low enough to love someone again. When you've been with someone or something for a significant amount of time, a sudden departure may leave you wondering how do you start all over again? This is also the case when we have been divorced from bondage. What used to have a hold on us may have been such a place of comfort that to redirect all our love and commitment to God at this point could become quite challenging. You may find yourself asking, *Where am I to start now?* One sure way I would quickly forget about a relationship I departed from was if the next one was good enough to make me forget about what I left behind. God's love is strong enough to make us forget what we divorced ourselves from. The problem is that many don't know how to fully tap into His love. After our divorce and after we have given our love over to God to be remade, He wants to give us lessons on what His love is really all about.

    The lessons that He taught me not only showed me how to love Him, but how to love others. Too many times in the past I have used the word *love* to describe my feelings for another. It wasn't until recently that I learned what it was all about. I had been in an ongoing relationship with a man for several years. This small word "love" became like a household term in our vocabulary because we used it so much. Looking back now I see how wrong we really were. It wasn't that love itself was wrong but rather the love we claimed to share with each other wasn't right. *The love we shared was not the love of God.* That's what happens to many couples who start off a relationship and forget to include God in it. So many people go to God on numerous issues in their lives. Yet, when it comes down to love and relationships they'll talk to strangers before they stop at His throne (as if He has no clue how to counsel His children on this subject.) I laugh at this because that is the same thing we have done or are still doing to our parents. Here we have people loaded with wisdom and insight but we sometimes refuse to tap into their knowledge until we have fallen on our faces. It took me a "fall" or two until I finally came to my senses and began to seek my Heavenly Father for guidance in this area. Love, was a subject that I had not yet mastered at one point in my life. I had to go to the one who has a Ph.D. in it. God with his mercy and grace did not fail me, flunk me, or give up on me. He merely taught me what I refer to as "love lessons". These are lessons that are essential to the growth and development of all those who claim to love Him.

<u>Lesson #1:</u> *There's only one love to live.*

    The first mistake that I made in past relationships was trying to love someone else with my own love and not with the love of Christ. I entered each relationship without bringing along the love instructor Himself. Because I did this, I held no regard for their needs. I was so driven by my needs that I overlooked the simple fact that I wasn't placed in their lives for my own pleasure, but for a purpose. There are single believers who feel that when they cross paths with someone else, if they "hit it off" on the first few dates, they can take a nose-dive into the lake of love. This is not always the case. In many instances, God just wants for that person to be ministered to.

    We should never think that every half-decent brother that we may "click" with is our mate. Not only can this get us into a lot of trouble but we could miss out on an opportune time of ministry. There is only one love to live and that love is the love of Christ. When we love someone with His love, we shouldn't have selfish motives for being with that person. When we love with Christ's love, we shouldn't look beyond their needs to find what will fill our voids. There is quite a difference between loving with our

Before I Do...I will

own love and loving with the love of Christ. No matter how "in love" we may think we are, if it does not match up with Christ's definition in 1Cor. 13, then we need to re-evaluate where our love is coming from. Is it patient, kind, long-suffering? Does it rejoice in iniquity or the truth? Does it bear all things, believe all things, hope all things, endure all things? Is it a love that never fails? If we possess the love of Christ then looking at someone as a brother or sister in Christ before looking at him or her as a potential mate should not be so hard. If we truly are exhibiting His love then finding out how God would have you to pour into that person's life before applying for a bridal registry should not sound foreign. We all need to begin to check our love and make sure that it is the kind of love that God can call His own.

<u>Lesson #2:</u> *Keep love all in the family.*

I have made the detrimental mistake in some of my past relationships of being unequally yoked with others. When I say unequally yoked I mean, of course, giving my love to unbelievers. We were not only on two different pages of life, we were on two different books when it came to our spirituality. The book I was on was the Lamb's book of life, which these brothers hadn't even subscribed to yet. I'm not saying that God cannot send a non-believer our way, then save him and bless us to marry him. Notice that I said my mistake was in giving these unbelievers *my* love. If we are to give any love it has to be the love of Christ, especially when dealing with unbelievers. The lesson to be learned here is to keep that love all in the family. Let these unbelievers feel the love of your Father, not your own love. Don't try to love unbelievers with a love outside of the one

God gives you. We are supposed to be leading these unbelievers to Him. If we let a selfish-motivated love get in the way, we will end up misleading them. When I tried to love these brothers I was driven to satisfy my own needs. It wasn't before long that I completely overlooked their need for God and His salvation. I made the mistake, as many believers do, of thinking that I could remain "saved" for myself and the brother I was involved with at that time. I felt that if I just remained who I was in Christ, these brothers would soon catch on and want to be in Christ too. The problem was in my struggle to remain who I was in Christ. I kept finding myself more and more out of fellowship with the same One I was trying to lead them to.

Being "unequally yoked" with someone is like traveling to a place we've never been with a person who doesn't speak the same language as we do. We may be able to kiss, hold hands, and even snuggle with that person but when it comes to pulling out the road map and actually getting to our destination, there may be some confusion along the way that will cause us to veer to the side of the road. The enemy would like to trick us into thinking that we can remain in these types of unbalanced relationships. I beg of you not to fool yourself. Learn from this love lesson and realize that you don't have to be in a relationship with someone to lead him/her to Christ. Our own selfish motives drive us to believe that. Yet, we *do* have to love everyone, with the love of Christ. If the love we are showing to others is not leading them to the Lord, we are not keeping love in the family. If we truly want to show love to someone, we should lead him/her to Christ and let Him draw him/her into a relationship with Himself. Let the love of God lead the way. If God has a plan for you to one day marry someone who is right now a non-believer, you'll have a

Before I Do...I will

better chance of seeing this come into fruition if you will learn to love with His love.

Lesson #3: *Don't awaken love until it pleases.*

Songs of Solomon is one of my favorite love stories written in the bible. Solomon and the young Shulamite woman reveal what true love is supposed to portray. The scripture that stands out to me the most is the one that says:

"I charge you daughters of Jerusalem, by the gazelles or by the does of the field, **do not stir up nor awaken love until it pleases"** **Sol. 2:7** (NKJV)

The Greek word for *please* is aresko. This means to be agreeable. Have you ever felt as though something between you and someone was "stirred up" but not agreeable unto the Lord? An example of this would be two believers who meet each other at church. They call each other up. They get to know each other. Next thing you know, they are inseparable. They feel this is safe for them because, after all, they are both saved. After a while, spending time alone becomes quite compromising for them spiritually. The hugging has turned into kissing. The kissing has become caressing. Need I go any further? Well, they go further and further and the next thing you know they wish they had never met. Now let's just say that the two of them were soulmates and marriage would not have been forbidden for them. Then why can they hardly bear to look at each other on Sunday in church service? *They stirred up love before it was agreeable to do so.*

There is a certain type of love that was only meant to be shared between a husband and wife. Many times that love is awakened way before its appointed time. We must not make this mistake. "Stirring up" love, before the right time, can be extremely detrimental. It can cause what was supposed to be a sacred and gratifying union to become a hasty and not so pleasurable division. The only time that love should be stirred between two people is when it is agreeable to the will of God. How can we tell? One way is by taking things slowly. The biggest mistake we can make in any relationship is rushing through it. Slow down so potential mistakes can more likely be caught before they happen. Take it slow by waiting for the Lord to reveal whether or not love should one day be "stirred up" with this person. Don't be so quick to make something out of a relationship. I remember when I tried to rush to make something on the stove one day. I threw the ingredients in a pot and turned on the heat. I stirred it all together only to find out later on, when I finally read the recipe, that half of the ingredients I used were not meant to be in that pot. What was I to do at that point? They were all stirred and mixed together. I had to throw it out and start over. This is what happens in many relationships. People jump into the relationship "pot" together, the heat is turned on, and instantly they try to "stir up" love. If they're not supposed to be with one another, a disaster can be made. Slow down and let God become the chef of your love life.

Lesson # 4: *Love should always bring you home.*

Remember the movie 'Boomerang' starring Eddie Murphy, Halle Berry, and Robin Givens. Well, for those of you who don't, Eddie Murphy played a character named Marcus Graham. Marcus was a true bachelor of the 90's. He had it going on. Intelligent, fine, and what some might

Before I Do...I will

call a "player". Dogging women was just one of the things he did quite well. Then when Marcus met Jacqueline, played by Robin Givens, he met his match. Everything he dished out boomeranged back to him. He was so "strung out" over Jacqueline that he could hardly see that there was someone that had come into his life, Angela, played by Halle Berry, that truly loved him. To make a long story short, Marcus eventually did notice and became quite close with Angela and the two of them moved in together. Yet his heart still belonged to Jacqueline. One night, he didn't come home to Angela because he was spending that night with Jacqueline. When he finally did come home, claiming how much he loved Angela, she said something that I thought was so powerful. "Love should have brought you home last night."

Some have spent many of their nights with relationships, goals, careers, etc. that have led them to leave God waiting for them to come home to Him. When we love with the love of Christ, His love should lead us home to Him every night and day. There is a famous cliché that says, "Home is where the heart is." God wants to dwell in the center of our hearts. If we are focusing too much on other things, we are not placing God in the center. If we put these things before the Lord and spend more time with them, we will end up neglecting Him. We may say we love God all we want, but the truth is spoken from within our hearts. God wants to feel assured that love will always bring us home.

These are only some of the love lessons God wishes for us to learn before marriage. Perhaps He is teaching you a few others. There is one more lesson I want to share that was quite a major lesson in my life. I feel this lesson is the most important of them all. I remember one conversation with God where He was telling me to give up one particular relationship with a guy I had been seeing for a couple of years.

"I can't do that, Lord," I cried, *"I need him to stay because I don't want him to be lost,"* I told Him in my Mother Theresa tone of voice. (This guy happened to be an unbeliever.)

God replied by saying, *"If you don't want him to be lost then let him go."*

At first I figured God just wasn't getting my point. However, God knew that I couldn't possibly have saved that man. It takes love to save someone, God's love, and I truly did not have it as I had thought. You couldn't tell me that I wasn't in love back then but God did.

He said to me one day, *"How can you say you love somebody and you don't know love?"* I was confused. *"I know what love is,"* I quickly retaliated.

"But you don't know Who love is," God said to me.

This struck me like a smack in the face. God told me that I could not possibly know what love was because I didn't know who *He* was. God is love. He did not only create it and give it; He is it.

How can we know what true love really is if we don't know Him? It is astonishing to me how many people are going around claiming to love one another but they don't know God. No wonder boyfriends are killing their girlfriends and wives are murdering husbands. No wonder mothers are putting little babies into garbage bags. We watch the news and say, *How can people be so cruel and cold-hearted, where is the love?* The love is in the Father. True love comes from up above.

I immediately knew after this conversation with the Lord that what He was saying to me was another lesson on love. The lesson I learned from this was before we can say we love *men* we have to come to know and love *Him*. Christ loves us very much yet we need to ask ourselves *are we showing love back to Him?* In the midst of your relationships with others, can the Lord say He feels loved by you? We show His ultimate love in our lives by putting Him first before anyone else. That is not to say that men can't love each other. We were made in the image of God so if He loves then we have the ability to love as well. Yet, in order for us to possess His true love, we must learn it from Him. We have to learn who He is in order for Him to unleash the full potential of what He has stored inside of us. Some of you may be in a relationship as we speak and you might be asking, *Is it wrong for me to love this person?* It is never wrong to love anyone. Jesus charges us to love one another. Yet, have you truly come to know the love of Christ so that you may give it to someone else? Loving with the love of Christ doesn't mean we are forbidden to look at someone as a potential mate. It is loving someone like Christ loves the church. It is caring for them enough to look beyond our own needs and desires. Our relationships, if Christ-centered, should exemplify Christ's love. If there is anything in our relationships that would compromise the purity, sincerity, and selflessness of that love, then we must question it.

What are the love lessons God is showing you? Whatever they are, God wants to use these lessons to change any wrong perceptions believers may have about His love. If He can change our perception about love, then

He can change how we may view Him. We will begin to see just how much He longs for us to fall in love with Him. Many of us have known about God for a very long time. Throughout our years we may have even grown to love Him. The question now is, *are we ready to fall in love with Him?* Many say they love Him and they know He loves them but they have never *fallen in love* with the Lord. There are those who have been in church all their lives, serving and praising the Lord, but have yet to experience Him as the Lover of their souls. He not only wants to teach us how to love Him but how to be loved by Him When you're ready to *love* someone you are ready to take who he/she is into your own arms. Yet, when you are ready to *fall in love* with someone you are ready to take who you are and place it in his/her arms. God has His arms wide open for you. Let Him show you how to fall in love with Him. Let Him teach you "love lessons" you will never forget.

Romancing the Stone

Let's talk about romancing the Stone. In other words, let's talk about falling in love and getting intimate with the Rock of ages, Jesus Christ. This "stone who the builders rejected" (Psalm 118:22) is the same one who wants to be the foundation of our love. A Greek word for *foundation* is katabole, which means the beginning or conception. He wants to be the first "stone" that is laid down in our hearts so that He may build His love in us. Whenever a structure has a weak foundation it is likely to lean or fall. Many couples in their relationships have swayed or have fallen because of a weak foundation. They didn't allow Jesus to lay down in their hearts. When love is built on His foundation, it will stand.

Before I Do...I will

Whenever a contractor begins to build he needs to uproot whatever is in the place where he wants to build. Then he can lay a proper foundation. He does not build on top of what is already in that place. God needs to remove what is already in our hearts so that He can build a proper foundation of love in us.

We allow Him to remove improper foundations when we begin:

(1) Trusting Him
(2) Giving ourselves totally to Him
(3) Letting go of the past
(4) Letting Him love away insecurities, fear, doubt, etc.
(5) Laying aside any hindrances to His love

We can allow God to remove any improper foundation within us when we take heed to these five steps. When He is the foundation of our love, not only will that love be able to stand in this season of singleness, but in any season that is to follow. In the book "Choosing God's Best"[3] Dr. Ron Rannikar stated "If current divorce rates continue, two out of three marriages that begin this year will not survive as long as both spouses live." There are so many failed marriages today. What was the foundation of these marriages? Their love couldn't have been built on Jesus.

The first step in learning to romance the Stone is making sure that the love within us is being built on the Lord. After we enter into a "contract" with God for Him to remake our love, then after He removes the improper foundations, only then can He begin to rebuild our love again.

God starts to build His foundation when we begin:

(1) Accepting His love into our hearts
(2) Being obedient to Him
(3) Loving Him with all our hearts, souls, minds, and strength
(4) Putting Him and His kingdom first
(5) Spending quality time with Him in prayer
(6) Staying committed to Him
(7) Expressing our hearts through worship and praise

After God rebuilds this foundation we are then ready to fall in love with Him. What does it really mean to fall in love with the Lord? When two people fall in love they embrace each other's love. Not only that, but they feel comfortable in each other's embrace. This is how God wants us to feel with Him. He wants us to feel at rest in His arms at all times. No matter how strong the winds of life are blowing around us we should feel safe in His embrace.

When someone falls in love he/she may also develop a strong desire to give of himself/herself. Whenever I really felt I was in love with someone, there was nothing I wouldn't give to that person. Being that I am a single believer, I later found out this type of giving was totally out of order. If we are not married we should not be giving all we have to anyone else, end of story. Yet, there is One to whom we can give our all to before we walk down the aisle. He is the one who longs for us to fall in love with Him. The Lord is calling for love from all those who are willing to give it.

In the story about the Samaritan woman when Jesus met that woman at the well the first thing out of His mouth was, *"Give me to drink"*. (John 4:7) The Lord wants a

Before I Do...I will

drink from us. He is thirsty for our hearts. It wasn't that Jesus wanted the water from the well when He met the Samaritan woman. That is not why He asked her for a drink. The reason He asked her for this drink was because He wanted what she had within herself that she was giving to everybody else but Him. Has there ever been a time that you gave yourself to everyone but the Lord? God is waiting to drink from us. He wants whatever we've been giving to everybody else. He's tired of waiting in the back of the line in our lives. A lot of people think the only time to go to Him is when they are in need. Have we considered that God *needs*? He needs a people that are not going to just seek His hands but seek His heart. He needs someone that is not just coming before Him to see what He can give them but what they can give Him. Being in a relationship with someone, who never comes to you except to collect something from you, can make you begin to hurt inside. Don't get me wrong, God loves to bless His people, but aside from that, He really longs for us to realize that sometimes He is calling us into His presence not just to answer every one of our needs but to whisper in our ears *'Give Me to drink'*.

    The drink that He longs to draw from us cannot be found in a well, but in *our will*. Just like that Samaritan woman drew from the well; it is our own "will" that we draw from everyday. God is thirsty for your "will" today. If He can capture a believer's will, then He can get that believer to completely turn his/her love over to Him. He will cause that believer to see that He is truly the Living Water. This "living water" inevitably satisfies. God is saying to us today what He said thousands of years ago to that Samaritan woman:

Nikki Simone

> *"If you knew the gift of God and who it is who says to you 'Give me a drink' you would have asked Him and He would have given you living water."* **John 4:10** (NJKV)

Will there ever come a time when every believer will become tired of reaching into his/her own will each day to satisfy his/her needs? God is not only asking us for a drink because He is thirsty; He also wants to satisfy our hearts. A woman with a satisfied heart is a woman who will drop her waterpot down to the ground and jump into the *river of romance* with her Savior.

Romance is simply a display of affection towards the one with whom you share an intimate relationship. The same way we would romance a spouse or a mate, we can turn that love over to God first. The thought of romancing the Lord may sound silly to some. Before I fell in love with Christ it sounded ridiculous to me. I felt like He was my Father and I could even refer to Him as being my friend, but a Lover? No way! The thought of me being this intimate with the Almighty was a bit much. When I ran across one of my first diaries and read one of the entries, I remembered why I changed my way of thinking. I had written about how I had been ignoring God that past weekend and all that particular day. I wrote how I knew it was nothing but the devil that caused me to behave this way because I really did long for a close relationship with Christ. I just used to go through periods in my life of just wanting to do my own thing. I knew that God was good and that He loved me, but every once in a while I would allow my flesh to overtake my spirit. This particular day as I was going throughout my day busying myself and doing everything in my will to not give in to the urge I was feeling to spend time with the Lord, I could hear Him

Before I Do...I will

clearly saying to me, *"Just five minutes. Just praise me for five minutes. That's all I am asking of you."* I was astonished. God was pleading for my time. It awed me that He in all His power and majesty would sound so desperate to commune with me. Curiosity and astonishment drove me to stop what I was doing and to lift up both my hands to begin praising Him. I hadn't gotten three words out before He began to speak to me again.

He said to me, *"Don't just say you love Me, show it"*. This line sounded too familiar. I used to say it all the time to the men that came in my life. *How could God be saying this to me?* He continued on to say, *"I don't want anybody to just tell Me they love Me, show it to Me. I need everything that every man and woman needs in a relationship. I need to be appreciated, loved, and cared for. I need to be paid attention to. All these things you need, I need them too."*

I couldn't believe how selfish and self-centered I had been towards God. I began to cry after He told me these things. I hadn't even realized it but I was withholding from Him what I needed for myself. I had no idea that He wanted these things from me so badly that He'd take the time to let me know personally. He's not a God without any emotional feelings. As I was crying, I could feel Him crying too. It was then that I knew that God was a God of emotions. He's a God that longs to be romanced by His people. One of the ways we can romance God is by giving him the opportunity to take a *drink* from us. He wants praise that will satisfy. He wants worship that will fill Him up. I've heard many times that the way to a man's heart is through his stomach. Well, the way to God's heart is through worship. It is through ultimate displays of affection from the ones He loves.

- How many times have we taken for granted that God needs to be appreciated, loved, and cared for?
- How often have we allowed Him to walk in and out of a room without taking notice that He was there?
- Do we as single believers allow thoughts of marriage, mates, and dating relationships to consume us to the point that we forget He wants to be the center of our attention?

Even if we don't consider ourselves guilty of doing any of these things, when we reach out for Him is it to take His hand or take from it? When I realized that God wanted a drink from my heart I began to ask what could I give Him. Right after the conversation that day I began to romance the Lord. We all can romance Him. Just begin to think what it is that you can do to show someone you care for him/her then give those things to God. Write down what you would do or say to someone to let him/her feel loved by you. For example, spending quality time after work instead of going out with friends. Writing poetry about the person then reading it out loud. There are so many things we can do to prove our love to God. He not only wants to be a part of our love lives; *He deserves to be.*

I don't know about you, but I made a commitment that I'm not only going to tell God I love Him, but I'm going to show Him. There was a time I was sad about not having a mate until I started treating God as if He were my mate. He once told me, *"If you will start treating me like I'm your man, I'll start showing you that 'I Am".* Are you willing to tell the Lord you're ready for His love? Are you ready to

Before I Do...I will

take out the time to love the One that is madly in love with you? I started coming into my apartment and speaking out loud to Him. As soon as I would come home I would shout *"Honey, I'm home"*. I would put down my purse, sit on my couch and ask, *"How was your day today"*. If you think that's crazy, I actually sat there and expected an answer from Him. I would run a bubble bath with candles all around and sing love songs to Him that I knew overwhelmed His heart. One day, I decided to have a picnic with Him, just Him and me. I set out the blanket, turned on my gospel love songs, and ate with my God. When I was all done eating, I laid on my back to look to the sky and communed with Him. I didn't even have to open my mouth and yet he heard every word. Now someone may think I'm nuts at this point. Several years ago, I would have thought so too. Yet, how can the love we have for God be real unless we show it? If the love I show the Lord can overwhelm His heart, then I'm willing to try. Nothing we do will ever compensate for what He has already done for us, but everything we do should at least say to Him, *Lord I love you.* Let Him lay the proper foundation of love in your heart. Then allow Him to show you ways to express your love for Him. Take out the time to romance your Stone today.

God's "Good thing"

I can somewhat relate to the Samaritan woman. She was going to draw water from a well that was full of water but none which could satisfy the thirsting in her spirit. She had been in relationship after relationship and still she was not satisfied. She even had a beau waiting at home for her, yet she still couldn't find anyone to quench her thirsts until she met Jesus. He was waiting there at the well for her. She had an appointment with Him and did not know it.

My satisfaction from the Lord started from an appointment I once had with Him. I was minding my own business, going throughout my normal day. I was about to dip into my own "will" again to satisfy a craving within my heart for love and there He was. He was standing near the edge of my will, waiting patiently for me. The Living Water leaned over and whispered ever so softly in my *ear 'Give Me to drink'*. I let go of my waterpot that day and began praising Him right there. As I was praising I began calling out His name. I called Him 'Master, Savior, and Deliverer.'

It was that very day He asked me *"When are you going to let Me be your lover?"* He said, *"You keep asking Me for a mate but I want to be your mate."*

I reminded Him, *"You're my Father and my Lord."*

He then said to me, *"Aren't I also your Everything?"*

"Well, yes," I answered.

"Then why can't I be your Husband?"

"For thy Maker is thine husband; the LORD of hosts is his name; and thy Redeemer the Holy One of Israel; The God of the whole earth shall he be called." **Is. 54:5** (KJV)

God wants to be the Lover of our souls and the center of our hearts. If He can be both our Mother and Father, or our Lawyer and the Judge, then why can't He be our Husband and Friend? He longs to caress us and to hold us in His arms. He rocks us to sleep at night and kisses us awake in the morning. He is madly in love with us. How can we continue to ask God for a mate if we haven't considered this love *He* has for us? That is like being in a

Before I Do...I will

relationship with someone that is constantly expressing his love to you, then asking him to introduce you to one of his friends.

This may all sound foolish thinking of God as a mate. *Can we really be wives to the Most High?* How? I was so curious at one point to know exactly how I could be a wife to God. He told me to write down everything that I thought it was going to take in order to be a good wife to my future mate. These are some of the qualities I wrote.

A good wife cleans
A good wife cooks.
A good wife is a good mother to her children.
A good wife is a good lover beyond just the bedroom.
A good wife is a strong support to her man.

God told me that all the things I think it will take to be a good wife for my mate are the same things it will take to be a good wife to Him. A lot of single believers have an idea of what it will take to make a good mate, but they have no idea that they don't have to wait until after their wedding day to show these characteristics. We should be expressing them to the Lord right now.

"The unmarried woman careth for the things of the Lord, that she may be holy both in body and in spirit..." **1Co 7:34** (KJV)

Before we can begin to be a wife to someone else, God is beckoning us to become His wife. Let's look at how we can begin to submit ourselves to God by breaking down the list I made.

- *A good wife cleans her house*. She keeps her household clean on a daily basis. No hardworking husband (or wife for that matter) wants to come in from a long, tedious day at work and not be able to find a place to rest because everywhere he turns there's a mess.

God also doesn't want to come home to this condition in our hearts. Our bodies are the temples of the Living God. He rests in our hearts. He is at work everyday, working on our blessings and promises. He is working on our situations. The last thing He wants to do is to come home to an unclean heart. The Lord is tired of coming home to a house where He supposedly has a key of residence but does not feel welcomed. We need to make sure that we do some "spring-cleaning" within ourselves. Remove all the dust balls of doubt. Sweep out any traces of sin. Throw out any trash that doesn't belong in your heart, mind, and spirit. The bible says:

"Jesus said unto him, Thou shalt love the Lord thy God with all thy heart, and with all thy soul, and with all thy mind." **Matthew 22:37** (KJV)

How can we be exhibiting this love to Him if we are not willing to keep these places clean for Him? There isn't anything God won't do for the woman who knows how to take care of His "house". In **Romans 12:1** it says:

"I beseech you therefore, brethren, by the mercies of God, that you present your bodies a living sacrifice, holy, acceptable unto God, which is your reasonable service." (NKJV)

Before I Do...I will

The Lord wants a wife with a clean temple that He can always come home to.

- *A good wife cooks for her husband.* She is a woman that cares about whether or not her husband is getting nourished everyday. She doesn't turn her back on him when she sees him going without. There is an innate desire within her to nourish her husband.

God feeds on our praise. He dines on our worship. His appetite is never ending. Everyday He is searching for that which is going to satisfy His craving within. Through prayer, praise and worship we nourish the heart of God. When the praises go up the blessings come down because God works overtime when his appetite is satisfied. The more we praise, the more the blessings keep flowing. God wants a wife who doesn't mind cooking up the praise that feeds His heart. He loves a woman who refuses to let her God be deprived or malnourished of the worship that nurtures Him. Regardless of what she is going through, a good wife will make sure that her husband's every need is taken care of.

- *A good wife is a good mother.* She would never abandon her children. Every good husband appreciates a woman that knows how to take care of his children.

God is expecting us to be good mothers to the children He births in us. Our ministries and spiritual gifts are the children He wishes to see us raise and nurture. He needs a wife that will attend to the cries of her ministry. He looks for wives who are willing to feed it with the Word when it becomes hungry. These women will clothe and protect their ministries with uncompromising righteousness. They accept them with open arms and loving hearts. If we are good mothers, there should be a bond between our ministries and ourselves that would make it difficult for us to walk away and leave them in the hands of someone else. We should want to take care of these ministries and watch them "grow up" so that they can be a blessing to the Body of Christ.

- *A good wife is a good lover*. She can love someone beyond the bedroom. She can love someone beyond the physical contact. T.D. Jakes said it best when he said that, "A lover is someone who can kiss your body and reach deeper to kiss your soul".[2]

God needs true lovers. He needs someone who doesn't just seek what He can physically do for her but one who seeks His face. These true lovers are whom He calls His true worshippers. They worship in spirit and in truth. They don't need any music or a choir. They freely worship from their hearts even in the toughest times of their lives.

- *A good wife is a strong support to the one she loves*. She stands behind her man. She listens to Him and follows his wise counsel. She believes in him.

God needs His wife to have total faith in Him. This woman will stand firm on His Word. She backs up His Word through her lifestyle. She is a living testimony of what He has spoken. This woman has an incredible way of embracing what the Lord has spoken to her and keeping it alive no matter what goes on around her. She carries whatever cross she has to bear for the sake of the kingdom of her Lord. I was once in thought about what kind of woman is attractive to God. He let me know that an attractive woman to Him is not the one who carries her purse, but carries her cross. She is the one who is a strong support to her Lord.

"Whoso findeth a wife findeth a good thing, and obtaineth favour of the LORD." **Proverbs 18:22** (KJV)

We have to *be* wives even before we can be found. God wants us to know that it is time for us to become blissfully married, while we are yet single. He wants our hands in marriage and He is reaching out to propose to our hearts. Aren't you tired of giving your heart to everyone else but Him? While we are married to Him, He can teach us the art of being a wife. He can teach us the lessons of His love that so many are too anxious to slow down and learn.

Often times my pastors preach the word of God as it pertains to the married couples of the church. I take that word and apply it to the marriage with my Husband, the Lord. I have read books that speak to married couples and I use many of the principles in those books as I apply them to Christ. Why should we wait until we have a mate to be taught how to be wives?

The best thing a high school can do for its students is to give them college prep courses. Even though these students are still in high school, they need to be prepared for that next level in their education. They may still have challenging times while in college, yet giving them a little preparation beforehand may go a long way. When we allow the Lord to be our Husband He can give us "marriage prep" courses to be better prepared for our mates. We are sure to

Nikki Simone

still have challenging times in our marriage, but the preparation God can give will help sustain us and enable us to excel in the long run.

Proverbs 18:22 was not talking about the already married woman. It was referring to the woman who had already determined in her mind that she was going to be a wife with or without a man in her life. Are we ready to be like this woman? Are we ready to be God's "good thing"? He has so much in store for us as a Husband. How can we pass Him by to jump in the arms of another? When you spend time with God giving Him what you are saving for your mate, He will honor that and bless the future He has for you. Whatever you think it takes to make a good wife, begin to give those things to the Lord. He'll show you what He can do in the life of a "good thing."

Pray this prayer with me today:

Dear Lord, I thank you for Your unfailing compassion towards me. Thank you for loving me the way You do. Now I'm asking You to help me to love You. Take my love into Your hands and remake it. I want You to bless, break, and multiply my love. Teach me Your "love lessons" that will enable me to love someone the way You do. I desire for You to be the foundation of my love. With my love built on You, I will surely know how to love and how to be loved by You. I drop, at this very moment, the waterpot that I have been using to dip into my own "will" and I am ready to 'give You to drink'. I jump into the river of romance with the Lover of my soul. Today I determine to be Your "good thing" before anyone else finds me. In Jesus' Name, I pray. Amen.

...I Will Help That Brother Find Me

He Don't Need Tips, He Needs A Waiter

Waiter, waiter! You forgot my order. Who's this? He's not what I ordered. I did? Well, I must have thought he was someone else. I want that guy over there instead. Wait! Come back here please. I changed my mind again. What about this one right here? I can just imagine how God must often feel when His children express their needs, wants, and desires for a mate. We probably sound as if we are giving food orders in a busy restaurant. *God I ordered that he needs to have a $75,000 a year job, not $35,000. Please take him away and bring me what I ordered.* It seems as though sometimes He is expected to prance around us addressing our every need, making every order match up just right with what we asked for. I thank the Lord that He is merciful or else many of us would have stopped being served a long time ago.

I have always been in the habit of leaving a tip for a good waiter. A good waiter is one who comes to your table on time. He checks on you periodically to see if you need anything extra. He is friendly, pleasant, and willing to serve you. Jesus has these very same qualities. He is the best waiter I know when it comes to serving His people. He not only checks to see what we need, He knows our needs before we sit down at the table. Imagine if every waiter already knew what we wanted before we sat down. We would save so much time looking through the menus trying to make a decision. God wants to save us some time today in our search through "the menu" for future mates. He already knows what we desire, He evens knows what is best for us. Now let me tell you how we can get it from Him.

There is nothing He ever brings us that is greater or smaller than what we need. He is an excellent waiter. When you have a really good waiter, if you stay seated at the table long enough, you will find that every part of your order will come out just right. If we stay in the presence of the Lord long enough we will see that everything He brings is just what we need. Though things may look like they aren't coming together we will begin to see that the "full course meal" is coming to completion right before our eyes.

"He who has begun a good work will be faithful to complete it." **Phil. 1:6** (NKJV)

When speaking about the service that the Lord gives, the problem does not lie within our "Waiter"; the problem arises when His customers don't want to *wait* on Him. This especially happens when some believers have to wait for a mate. Instead of sitting at the Lord's table (presence) some would rather go to one of the fast food "joints" on that issue. They don't think they have the time and patience to sit down in the presence of God and wait for Him to serve them a "well-done" man. They are more apt to settle for the "medium-rare" brother with some fries and a coke. Instead of waiting on the Lord, they would rather hear Him say *"Coming right up"*. We'll never have the best of what God wants for us this way.

I used to be a complaining customer in the presence of God. I shouted orders of what I wanted and how I wanted it not realizing that my "Waiter" had my best interest at heart. I was so hungry for more than what appeared to be on the place mat in front of me. One thing I've learned

Before I Do...I will

since then is that God is not in the business of short changing the ones He loves. He wants us to have everything that can fit on our plates. In fact, He wants to bless us with more than that. (Eph. 3:20)

Though God is an excellent waiter, *tips* are not what He needs from us when it comes time for Him to bless us with mates. He doesn't even need us to constantly remind Him what's on the menu. What He really needs is for us to learn to wait. The word "wait" has two basic meanings. The first one, of course, is being patient; waiting with expectation. Patience represents a level of faith that is ever so pleasing to God. Every believer should exhibit patience when he/she is waiting on God to do something for him/her. Yet, I want to deal with the second meaning of wait, which means being a servant. The Greek word for *wait*, prosedreuo, means to sit near; attend as a servant. Proskartereo is another Greek word for wait. This word means to persevere or to be constantly diligent, adhering closely as a servitor. **Lamentations 3:25** says:

"The Lord is good unto them that wait for him, to the soul that seeketh him." (KJV)

God not only wants us to be patient. He also wants us to wait on Him, as in serving Him. Here are several scriptures that concern waiting on the Lord.

Ps 25:3 *"Indeed, let no one who waits on You be ashamed..."* (NKJV)

Ps 25:5 *"Lead me in Your truth and teach me, for You are the God of my salvation; on You I wait all the day."* (NKJV)

Nikki Simone

Ps 37:34 *"Wait on the LORD, and keep His way, and He shall exalt you to inherit the land; when the wicked are cut off, you shall see it."* (NKJV)

Ps 104:27 *"These all wait for You, that You may give them their food in due season."* (NJKV)

Is 40:31 *"But they that wait upon the LORD shall renew their strength; they shall mount up with wings as eagles; they shall run, and not be weary; and they shall walk, and not faint."* (KJV)

If God were to ask each of us are we willing to wait on Him there would probably be a resounding 'yes' ringing in our hearts, yet are our hearts matching up with our actions towards Him? Let's picture for a moment God sitting down at a table. If He were to judge the way we are *waiting* on Him right now would He be pleased with the kind of service that we are giving unto Him? If there was one thing that displeased me in any restaurant, it was when my waiter was so busy trying to serve other tables that he neglected to check on mine. If it took him too long to come back to my table I would get upset. When we serve God we have to make sure that we are not so busy trying to serve at other "tables" that we neglect where He is seated. Even if those tables appear to be church related activities such as auxiliaries, ministries, conferences, etc., nothing can take the place of the table of the Lord's presence. We should spend more time at His table than the others.

Some of these other tables can consist of our jobs, people, relationships, goals, and the list goes on and on. God is lifting His finger our way and softly calling us over to His table. *Waiter!* In the midst of all these things He is trying to gain our attention. Are we giving Him enough of our service, or do we keep passing Him by as we run to serve something or someone else? Or, are some of us still trying to grab His attention to cater solely to our needs? I cannot imagine myself sitting in a restaurant then my waitress coming over to me with her pen and pad and sitting herself across from me to tell me what she wants and needs. I am not saying that God does not want to hear our needs and desires.

"Be anxious for nothing; but in everything by prayer and supplication, with thanksgiving, let your requests be made known to God." **Phil. 4:6**

There is nothing wrong with voicing our needs and desires, yet He already knows His plan for us. He does not need any tips on how to bless us or who to bless us with. What He really needs is a waiter. He needs someone who will trust Him enough to forget about his/her own desires to serve His. How do we serve God's desires? By attending to and being obedient to His will. We serve His desires when we constantly come to His "table" to carry out what He desires from us.

If we never effectively learn how to cater to God's needs, how will we then be able to faithfully and diligently cater to the needs of a future mate? As wives of the Living God, we have to begin to wait on our Lord. He has need of us all. Just like He asked of the Samaritan woman, He is asking of every one of His waiters, 'Give Me to drink'. Let Him know that you have the *water* He is thirsting for. God is not beckoning us to serve Him because He's tired. He's not on a break. When God makes a request for us to give something to Him it is undoubtedly a setup. He is asking us to bring everything He's ordering straight to the table of His presence. If we do this without ceasing it won't be before long that He will sit us down at His table and cause us to see that every order we brought unto Him was a part of His setup to bless us. He needs a *waiter*. Give Him what He orders.

How'd She Get Her Boaz

The first time I read the story of Ruth in the bible I have to admit that I wanted to find her and ask how'd she get her Boaz and why was it that nothing like that has ever happened to me. It seemed as though the harder I tried to search for my Boaz the more I ended up with nothing but Bozos. There were many times that I felt I was running a "soul" circus with all the clowns I've encountered in my life. How was it that this woman just waltzed herself right into Boaz's backyard? I definitely had to read this story a couple of times before I could catch on to how she did it.

The story starts off by explaining how this young girl married one of the two sons of Elimelech and Naomi. After some time, Naomi's husband and two sons died and Naomi headed back to her hometown of Judah. While on her journey back to Judah, Naomi beckoned her two daughters-in-law to go back home but Ruth refused to go back. Ruth went to Judah with Naomi and there dedicated her service to her bereaved mother-in-law. While serving Naomi, Ruth came upon the field of a wealthy and prestigious man named Boaz. When he took notice of her he blessed her with much favor. Eventually, Naomi gave Ruth advice on how to propose to this man. By listening to Naomi, Ruth later became the great-grandmother of King David and was also in the direct lineage of Jesus Christ.

Ruth was not the only one who has ever come upon a good mate. There are many couples today who I look upon

Before I Do...I will

and wonder if I'll ever be as blessed in my marriage with my future mate. Though I do believe that I can be so blessed, God had to let me know that there was a method to procuring a "Boaz". Some feel that all they have to be is pretty or have a nice body to get this kind of man. Some feel an education is all they need. While others seem to think that the true way to any man's heart is through his stomach. These things may hold true if you are looking for a Bozo, but if you are looking for a "Boaz", you have got to be a "Ruth". In other words, there are certain godly and virtuous characteristics that Ruth possessed that are needed to attract the attention of the Boaz we desire. Here are the three ways Ruth got her man.

Ruth served.

The first thing that I noticed about Ruth was how diligently she served or "waited on" her mother-in-law, Naomi. She was definitely a "waiter". Ruth expressed such a selfless and humble servitude towards this woman. Despite the fact that both Naomi and Ruth had lost their husbands, Ruth didn't allow her situation to hinder her from seeing that someone else was in need.

Regardless of the situations that may occur in this season of our lives, someone else has need of us. There is something that God put inside of each of us that He sends other people to draw from. Many people come in our paths, not by coincidence, but because of what God has put inside of us to share with them. Ruth had a comforting spirit that eventually brought Naomi out of her state of depression and despair. Let's imagine for a moment if Ruth had left Naomi during their journey to return to her own country and home. Not only would she not have met Boaz, but the one who was in need of her, Naomi, may have never been able to rise above this desolate demeanor that held her captive. God honors the woman who puts the needs of others before her own. Serving others in the godly and virtuous way that Ruth served Naomi is likened to serving the Lord. He honors this kind of service as though we are giving it to Him directly. Real joy comes from putting God's needs and then the needs of others before our own.

<u>Ruth was willing to leave things behind</u>.

Another characteristic I noticed about Ruth was her willingness to leave behind her life in order to give to someone else. Ruth dedicated her life to serving Naomi. She left behind all she had back home and went to the place where Naomi dwelled. Sometimes serving others may call for us to leave behind the familiar places of our lives. When God called me to serve my pastor, at first it was somewhat awkward for me. I found it challenging to focus on the needs of someone other than myself. I could have chosen to stay in the place where I didn't have a care in the world. I could have decided that I wanted to stay free from serving and helping another. Yet, like Ruth, I made a decision to come from out of the place where I once dwelled.

It takes courage and a willing spirit to leave behind the old in order that God may take you to a new place in Him. That's what Ruth did when she refused to leave her mother-in-law to go back home. We have to be willing to leave things behind if we want a "Ruth blessing". These places can include our pasts, our old mind-sets, relationships, etc. In my case it was a selfish nature that I had to leave behind. What is God calling you to leave behind in order to serve?

Before I Do...I will

<u>Ruth was obedient and followed counsel</u>.

Naomi gave Ruth instructions to follow in order to get Boaz to marry her. There are many women today who have so much wisdom to offer young women when it comes to acquiring and keeping a mate. We, like Ruth, have to be willing to receive their wise counsel with open hearts and minds then be equally willing to follow through with that counsel. Ruth did all that Naomi told her to do and ended up with a blessing she could not have anticipated. She didn't say, *Naomi doesn't know what she's talking about. It's been so long since she had to find someone.*

One of the biggest mistakes that many young people make today is that they don't listen to wise counsel. A lot of their mistakes can possibly be avoided if they will learn to heed the words of those who try to counsel them. I especially make it my priority to listen to the Naomi in my life. If she tells me to go left, I go left. If I am to go right, that is where I'll go. I simply repeat in my heart the words that Ruth said to Naomi after she was given instructions on how to propose to Boaz, *"All that you say to me I will do."* We can throw our lives and purpose off course by not listening to the Naomi God has placed in our paths. If Ruth had not listened to Naomi, she would not have been in the direct lineage to Jesus. If you haven't done it already, find yourself a Naomi who you can be accountable to during this season of your life.

When Ruth made a decision to serve her mother-in-law, she didn't have an ulterior motive in mind such as meeting someone or looking out for herself. She had no idea when she walked on Boaz's field to glean from his crops that she was walking into her next season. When we really make up in our minds that we are going to serve the Lord with all our hearts, that is when He decides that we are ready for the next season in our lives. When we walk away from our own will, we get right on the pathway to our next blessing. It interested me that the place where Ruth served someone else was, in essence, the place where her mate found her.

- Could it be possible that your future mate is going to look for you in the place of service God is calling you to?
- Could the reason that "Boaz" is difficult for many to find be because they are too busy looking for him to stop and serve someone else?

God never asked us to look for our mates. All He asks of us is to be in the place of service that He has called us to. Ruth did not have to look at all. *She stepped right into her blessing when she determined in her heart to serve.* She could have still been in mourning for her deceased husband. She could have been longing for those warm arms that once embraced her. Instead, she wrapped her arms around someone else and embraced them in their time of pain.

Who is God placing in your life at this time to serve? Is it a family member or friend? Is it your pastor or a member of your church? Could it be a co-worker or even someone who is a complete stranger? What place is He sending you to in order that you may forget about your current situation to become a blessing? Ask the Lord, if He has not already made it clear to you, where Naomi is in your life. Then ask for divine wisdom in order to serve from your heart. Naomi does not necessarily have to be a woman but rather someone or something that is in need of the service that you have inside of you. There is a good chance that your

Before I Do...I will

Naomi is not far from the next place where God would like to bless you.

I'm not suggesting that you go find your Naomi simply for the purpose of finding your mate. Yet if you serve your Naomi with the sincere attitude and diligence that Ruth served with, God will move you closer to the place of your blessing. Does this mean that Boaz will find you right away? Not necessarily. You may still feel as though everyone is passing you by to get married. That's okay. Never get discouraged or upset with someone else who has found her Boaz. I have learned to rejoice with my sisters who God has blessed with mates. The bible says:

"Rejoice with those who rejoice..." **Romans 12:15**

Every single sister who is waiting for God to bless them with a mate should read the story of Ruth and be encouraged. The next time you look at someone else and find yourself asking, *"How'd she get her Boaz?"* remember the qualities that Ruth possessed and how her story ended. A humble spirit, diligent servitude, courage, obedience, and virtue are only some of the qualities Ruth possessed that brought this woman straight to Boaz's door. What qualities and characteristics do you possess that will catch the attention of a Boaz? If they are not anything like the ones Ruth possessed, WATCH OUT! You may just receive a Bozo in disguise.

Shopping Wisely For What We Want

There are three major mistakes that people make when they shop unwisely; they put things in their carts that they don't need, they forget to pick up the things they really needed, and they overspend. This may not be such a big deal in a supermarket but in life we cannot afford to be unwise shoppers, especially in terms of finding a mate. (When I talk about finding a mate I am not talking about going out and searching for one. Again, I want to reiterate that that is not God's intention for the single woman. Yet, for the purposes of this chapter I will use the term "mate finding" as I explain how to shop for what we want in a mate.)

Being unwise in our mate-finding can cause us to pick up what we don't need in a mate, leave behind what really matters, and pay a price that is way more costly than we could ever anticipate. Many people question how they are to know when they have found the right mate. In order to find the answer to that question, we have to learn to be wise shoppers. Whenever we go into any supermarket it would behoove us to be wise if we want to walk away satisfied. The same rule applies in our search for mates. Here are the do's and don'ts that every believer should take heed to before he/she walks into the "mate-market" season of his/her life.

Do's:
Do pray before you shop around.
Do make a list.
Do check the produce.
Do bring your coupons.

Do pray before you shop around.

In the 24th chapter of Genesis it talks about Abraham wanting to find a wife for his son, Isaac. Abraham made his servant vow not to pick a wife from the daughters of the

Before I Do...I will

Canaanites but rather to go to his country and family to chose a wife there. After his servant made this vow, he faithfully journeyed to find Isaac a wife. The servant ended up at a well and *prayed* to God for favor and guidance in his search. It was imperative for the servant to pray for guidance. He was at a well and being that it was the custom for the women to be the ones to draw water for their families, many women came to that well. He needed to be able to decipher which woman to choose. His problem would not have been finding a woman but he needed the *right* one.

It would be foolish in our quest for mates not to pray for guidance. There are many believers that come to the Spring of Life, Jesus Christ. Which one is right for you? How are you to know? By praying for guidance you can eliminate much confusion. Prayer is so important when your blessing time is near. Before Abraham's servant was finished praying, the answer to his prayer, Rebekah, was heading towards the well with her pitcher on her shoulder. God has our answers even before we begin to pray. Prayer draws the answer to the need.

Do *make a list.*

I can remember a statement someone made during a "girl-talk" discussion I was involved in with a group of friends and close relatives. This person stated that part of the key to happiness in a marriage is knowing what you want before you walk down the aisle. After we have prayed for God to direct our steps, the next thing to do is to get a pen and pad out so that we can make a list of the characteristics we would like to see in our mates. Many people get married first and then hope the list of things they didn't want in a mate is not too long. That can be unnecessarily risky. It is a proven fact that if you know what you want before you shop for it, you'll spend less time in the store and you'll be more likely to come out satisfied.

Everyone should have a list written concerning the type of mate and relationship they desire. Why? Simply because, if we don't know what we want, everything can begin to look appealing. Just like in a supermarket we may start grabbing for whatever is near just because it looks good.

The second thing that can happen is that we can become so indecisive that we pass every good thing by. Have you ever been really hungry walking through a food court when everything smells and looks so good to you? I have walked around in circles many times, indecisive about what I really wanted. By the time I made my final decision, being exhausted, I would choose what I wanted the least. Every time this happened I wanted to kick myself for not knowing ahead of time what I wanted. When I finally started making a list, the description of the mate I desired became clearer to me. I stopped grabbing for whoever was near me and I was determined not to let who I truly needed pass me by. If any man was going to be for me, I would know it not only from being in line with the will of my Father but also because a lot of his descriptions would need to be on my list.

Do I actually mean for us to sit down, put on our thinking caps, and get honest with ourselves as we write down exactly what we want? I sure do. I used to think that we should have a list so that we can apprise God of exactly what we want. I later realized that this list is not for God at all (He already knows). Rather this list is for ourselves so that we don't fall into the temptation to pick up what we don't need. If you have a list you are more likely to pick up the ingredients for the type of mate you need and desire. If I need to make a lasagna dinner I would not go around putting ingredients for chicken noodle soup in my cart. I would look at my list and pick up only the ingredients that are going to help me get what I want.

Here are some of the questions that should help you start off your list. I am sure you may be able to come up with many more of your own.

- What characteristics do I want in a mate?
- Which ones do I not want?
- What are some of the qualities I feel he should have in order to be considered a good husband, father, etc.?
- Out of all these qualities what are the top ten, five, and three that are most important to me?
- What is the number one important characteristic that my mate should possess?
- What kind of relationship will make me happy?

Make your list today. Then pray again to the Father to make sure that everything on your list can match up with His will for you. He will show us what needs to be on our lists so that we can avoid making wrong choices during this season.

Do *check the produce.*

When I go into a produce section in a supermarket I never just grab a piece of fruit and throw it in my cart. I check it first. I make sure it's not rotten or spoiled. If it is, I throw it back and proceed to check the next one that I pick

Nikki Simone

up. Neither should we just pick up what appears to be a mate and carry him around in our hearts without checking to make sure he is producing good fruit. So many people are guilty of grabbing someone first then checking him/her out once they get that person home. That's when they find out that the person's spirit is rotten to the core. If we want the best God has for us, we have to use the common sense He blessed us with. The bible tells us in **Matthew 7:16**:

"You will know them by their fruits." (NKJV)

God does not want us to play a guessing game when it comes to choosing His best for us. If ever we are considering someone as a potential mate we should ask ourselves what fruits are we being shown? **Matthew 7:17-18**:

"Even so, every good tree bears good fruit, but a bad tree bears bad fruit. A good tree cannot bear bad fruit, nor can a bad tree bear good fruit." (NKJV)

It would be foolish for us to pray and ask God whether someone is the right one for us if we can visibly see how rotten his fruits are. That would be like picking up an apple that is so rotten that it has turned brown then going to the courtesy counter to ask them, D*o you think I should buy this?* Check the produce before you make a choice about a mate.

Do *bring your coupons.*

The first time God told me to pray for my husband, I remember thinking *what husband?* He said, *"The one I'm*

Before I Do...I will

going to give to you." There are many times during this season in my life that I pray, not for *a husband*, but for *my husband*. I pray for his salvation, his ministry, and his relationship with the Lord. I also pray for our future together. I speak blessings over our household and our children. I prophesy that he will be a good husband, father, etc. There are so many prayers you can pray into the life of your future mate even if you do not know whom you are going to marry. I took God literally because I believe that if we speak something into existence even before we see it, we shall have it.

These prayers that I pray are like coupons that I will need to carry into the "mate-market" with me. Coupons may seem as though they are small and insignificant pieces of paper. However, if you bring enough of them to the cash register, when it is time to purchase your items, they can be used to save you quite a bit of money. By the same token, the prayers that we pray as singles may seem as though they are bouncing off the walls of our living rooms, but if we pray fervently, these prayers can be used to save our marriages before they begin. The bible tells us:

"The effective, fervent prayer of a righteous man avails much." **James 5:16** (NKJV)

Many spend a significant amount of time just praying for a mate. Yet, they don't bother to pray *for* that mate. What we need to pray for is our futures with the mates that God wants to bless us with. Also, we need to pray for ourselves, that our mates will find us to be virtuous women. We should pray for ourselves to become the kind of wives to our mates that will please God. Prayer makes a difference. Take time to ask God how you should pray for your mate. Please don't pray for someone else's mate. God will never honor a prayer for a married man. Also, if you are calling out the name of someone specifically, you should first make sure that God told you he's the one you will marry.

Don'ts:
Don't ever enter a market if you have not eaten.
Don't be foolish enough to take what you did not pray for.
Don't leave home without checking your list twice.
Don't be a shoplifter and think you won't get persecuted

***Don't** ever enter a market if you have not eaten.*

We do it all the time. We go into a supermarket on an empty stomach then cringe as the cash register reveals the price we have to pay. I once put so much in my cart while I was shopping that I had to tell the cashier to void out almost half of my items. I picked up way more than I needed but I couldn't help myself. I was so hungry that even the non-food items looked appetizing to me. What's worse is that I had so much "junk food" in my cart that I didn't seem to notice what I really needed was missing. When it came time for the cashier to put half of those items back, I found most of what was left for me to purchase were the things I craved for rather than what would nourish me.

By the same token, we cannot afford to shop for a mate on an empty heart. That is why it is so important to establish our love with Christ first. If we are looking for a mate without taking the opportunity to indulge in a solid, gratifying relationship with the Lord, our actions will become quite costly. Not only that, but we will end up paying a price for what we didn't really need. We are likely to make many unwise choices on an empty heart. We can't think straight if our hearts are empty. Before we enter the "market" we have to make sure we allow God to fill us with His love. He can nurture our hearts.

Don't *be foolish enough to take what you did not pray for.*

I can't understand how believers get married who have not asked God whether or not they were making the right choice. Whenever I ask God to lead me to the right bargains in a store, I always end up saving money. How much more will He be willing to save our marriages? God hates divorce. He hates division but loves unity. There is nothing He would desire more for you and your future mate then for the two of you to dwell together in unity.

There are so many believers who are now married that have said *if only I had asked God first*. If we fail to ask for guidance in our search for mates, we may suffer as a result. Don't pick up what you didn't pray for. To exclude God out of the decisions we make for our mates can be dangerous. Mate finding is such a crucial decision making time that we cannot afford *not* to include God in it. When we pray first and include God in what we do, we are authorizing Him to direct our paths. (Prov. 3:6) He needs to be right there with us every step of the way.

Don't *leave home without checking your list twice.*

When we come to a point in our seasons where we have to check our lists to make sure a person is right for us, not only should we check our list once, but twice. We are to check the list once to see if the one who we are considering matches up with our lists, then a second time to make sure that *we* match up with our own lists. If one of the qualities you want in a mate is someone who has a deep intimate relationship with Christ, ask yourself how solid is your relationship with God. If you put on your list that one of the qualities you don't want in a mate is someone who doesn't know how to manage his finances, ask yourself how have you been proving yourself as a steward financially. If you are looking for someone to be an excellent father, what are some of the qualities you possess to show you can be a good mother?

When you are checking your list don't forget to get your own self in check. Many people want mates but they don't take out the time to first work on themselves. They go into their marriages incomplete. Two halves don't make a whole when it comes to marriage. It is God's intention for two whole people to come together as one.

Don't *be a shoplifter and think you won't get persecuted*

Not only do we have to be wise but we must also remember that all shoplifters will be persecuted. What do I mean by that? A shoplifter would be a person who tries to take what they did not pay a price for. We pay a price for a satisfying marriage through our willingness to be patient and obedient during our season of singleness. We become shoplifters when we begin to grab for things we didn't pay for with our patience and obedience to God. We put things in our hearts that don't belong to us and we walk right out into our future, fooling ourselves into believing we are

Before I Do...I will

going to be blessed that way. Let us not forget that there is One who watches over us that is far more advanced then any security camera. We might make it through that front door and into the rest of our lives but persecution will come when we get that man home and find out that he's the wrong one. Or, when we find that he needed more time on the "shelf" before we snatched him up.

We may find that we were so quick to get these brothers home that though they looked as though they fit the descriptions on our lists, it was nothing but their false advertisements that caught our eyes. We must be careful when it comes to our lists. When we come into the knowledge of what we want so does the devil. He will place someone on the shelf that looks, sounds, and acts like what we have on our lists. If we don't pay the price of patience and obedience, we will later find that we picked up someone who only *appeared* to have what we needed.

There are many more do's and don'ts when it comes to shopping for what we want in a mate. Please don't ignore them. If we are wise shoppers in a supermarket we are more likely to walk successfully through the aisles. Likewise, being wise shoppers in the "mate-market" will enable us to walk successfully down the aisle to the ones God has for us.

Have we met?

One of the problems that can occur if we rush through our season of singleness is that we can end up not giving God enough time to complete us. Many go into marriages incomplete. They didn't stay in the hands of the Lord long enough for Him to mold them and make them suitable for marriage. If we look closely at how God made Eve we can then begin to understand His "making" process. First, God made Adam. He spent time alone with Adam. There was no one else on the scene to distract them from their quality time together. Somewhere along the line He decided that Adam needed a helpmeet. That is when He put Adam to rest. He took out one of Adam's ribs to create a helpmeet for him. Notice that after He took Adam's rib out, He did not wake Adam back up and say, *Hey look man, I want you to watch me make your wife. Isn't she beautiful? How do you like her so far?* He allowed Adam to stay asleep. Why? I believe it was because He wanted to spend time alone with Eve as well. After He formed her mouth, He wanted to be the One to kiss her awake with His breath of life. After He formed her arms, He wanted those arms to wrap around His embrace before they would reach out to someone else. He wanted to be the first to whisper in her ears how beautiful she was.

There is no doubt that God wishes to spend time alone with each one of us while we are single. He does not want any distractions while He is making us complete. He does not want us to run off into relationships with others before He has had a chance to have quality time alone with us. Our Lord longs to be the One that awakens us with kisses every morning. He desires to be the One that we wrap our love around first before all others. *Are we allowing Him to have the quality time with us that He longs for?* In the lives of every single believer, God wants to establish a love covenant with us before we establish one with anyone else. He wants to reveal to us what true love is supposed to feel like. For the single believers who He will give the gift of marriage to share with someone else, He wants to take this quality time a step further by using that time to complete us

Before I Do...I will

for the mates He will bless us with. God wants to make you recognizable to the "Adam" He has for your life.

If we look at the story of Adam and Eve we will see that Adam noticed Eve as soon as he laid eyes on her. He not only noticed her but he recognized her. There was something about her that was familiar to him. Although Adam was sleeping while God took out his rib to form Eve, when he saw her he recognized that she had what was missing inside of him. In the bible he refers to Eve as bone of his bone and flesh of his flesh. (Gen. 2:23) Adam could have petted her head as if she were one of the many creatures that God allowed him to name in the garden. Yet, there was something about this girl that was different from anything else in the garden. There were no mirrors in Eden and still Adam knew that Eve was a reflection of him. She was a compliment to him who needed no introduction.

There is something God wishes to put inside of us that will be identifiable to the mate He has for us. If ever there comes a time that we are considering someone for marriage who matches up with the characteristics shown on our lists, the questions we then need to ask ourselves are:

- Am I recognizable to him?
- Do I remind him of himself?
- Does he possibly overlook me because he does not notice me?

God could have formed Eve with her own set of ribs apart from the one He took from Adam's body, but that was not in His plan. If He is fashioning you for an "Adam" He will use a part of that man to help form you. Check the qualities that God is trying to cultivate in you during this season. Chances are that those are the "ribs" that God is pulling out of your future mate. If so, our quality time with God is extremely important because it is through that time that we allow Him to deposit these qualities in us that are needed by our mates. If Eve, mid-way through her "making", had become preoccupied with someone or something else so that she did not allow God to spend this quality time with her, she would not have received what Adam needed in her.

Many single women today do not allow God to complete them. Mid-way through their "making" they become distracted by someone or something. They jump out of the arms of the Lord and run off to these distractions. They come back to God huffing and puffing, asking Him, *Where's my mate, Lord? I'm still single. How long do I have to wait?* I can imagine God responding to them, *When are you going to allow Me to finish putting these qualities in you so that I may present you to your mate? If I present you now, how is he supposed to recognize you?*

Even if you have already met the one who is supposed to be your future mate, he can pass you right by if he doesn't recognize you as his wife. There were times when I ran off in other relationships with men that I knew I was not going to marry. I did this because I just wanted the thrill of being with someone while I waited for God to send me my mate. I didn't realize at the time that I was prolonging the process. I wasn't allowing Him to instill these essential qualities and characteristics in me (the ribs).

When God begins making us ready for a mate, He is making us the "donor" for his needs. If we get married we should be much more than wives to our husbands, we should also be the donors that hold their vital necessities inside of us. It is very disturbing when two saved people go to their pastor and get all the wrong counseling about marriage, if any at all. The pastor says things such as, *Hey you're saved; he's saved. It's a perfect match. Get married and be happy.* Just because two people are saved doesn't mean that they are the ones for each other. Then this couple gets married and finds out that everything is wrong.

Marrying someone all wrong for us is like needing a kidney transplant and receiving one from the wrong donor. If the couple doesn't go to God to help them fix up the mess, there can be a rejection that takes place similar to a person's body rejecting the wrong kidney. This "rejection" can lead to separation and divorce. Why go through all of that when we can have the right donor the first time? If God presents us to our mates we should be so familiar to them that they almost have to stop and ask *'Have we met'? 'Haven't we seen each other before?'* If God brings us together with our mates it should be as though we have always been together. I'm not saying that this should authorize us to jump right into a marriage and skip over laying down a foundation as friends first. There is still no need to rush a relationship, especially when someone is the right one for us.

It is one thing for God to not be finished with you and keep your blessings on hold until you are ready for them, yet it is another thing for you to not let God be finished with you because you were not where He could complete you. We can miss many blessings this way. Let God instill the qualities (ribs) in you that will awaken your Adam from his rest. Don't be surprised if you hear the words *'Have we met'*.

Nikki Simone

Adam's not dead, he's just resting

Many believers, if they are not careful, begin to think that something is wrong with them as their years of singleness go by. Yet, there is a process that comes before any prosperous marriage can begin. A good parent makes a child wait for what they want because they know there are things that must be put in priority. Whenever my mother would make one of her delicious apple pies, she would sit it right on top of the stove as the aroma flirtatiously lured the whole household into the kitchen. Yet, no matter how good that pie smelled, looked, or would potentially taste, she would never let any of us just dive right into it. We all knew that there was a meal being prepared for us that had to be completed before eating dessert. We could beg her and try to bribe her all day but we knew no matter what we did or said we had to wait.

God, being the good parent He is to us, operates this same way. He makes us wait until our preparation is done. We have to wait not only until He is finished preparing us, but He wants us to wait until our mates are fully prepared as well. If we indulge in marriage before God approves, the end result might be as unpleasant as the stomachache that comes from eating dessert before dinner.

Going back to the story of Adam and Eve in Genesis, we can see how God prepared each one. He prepared Eve by taking her in his hands, making and molding her into what would best suit Adam. He prepared Adam by putting him to rest. God taught me that when He begins to prepare a mate for His daughters, He puts that man to rest. This can be a very frustrating time for the single woman who is waiting because when someone is resting they are not moving. They actually look dead. I sometimes wanted to tell God, *"Lord, at least let me see him breathing."*

I wanted to see some movement during the lonely times I had to endure in this season but there was none at all. The telephone didn't ring. The doorbell didn't buzz. No gentleman on the street stopped to acknowledge me by saying 'hello'. I felt like no one was interested in me. In fact, there were times when no one even looked my way. Not even the "home-boys" looked my way to shout their usual "hey shorty" salutations. I know someone reading this right now can relate to what I'm saying. If we are not watchful, we can become depressed during this season.

I remember when someone gave me a prophecy that I was going to get married. All "hell" broke loose in my singleness. I felt like going back to that person and begging them not to ever mention the "m" word to me again. It can become quite frustrating to wait. Even if we are delighting in the Lord this does not mean that the temptations of marriage will not try to fester in our hearts.

I began to feel unwanted and rejected until the Lord reminded me that Adam is not dead, he's just resting. I want to take this time to encourage those who feel that God has promised them the gift of marriage. You may be doing all that you know to do to delight yourself in the Lord and abide in His holy word. You may feel that you are proving yourself to be uncompromisingly righteous by putting God first and foremost in your life. Yet, you may also feel that it wouldn't hurt to have a mate by your side, especially if the Lord has already made it known to you that He has a mate for you. Don't be discouraged. *God has put your Adam to rest.* You may not see any "movement" in your singleness but God is ordering every one of your steps. The Lord has a way with taking a situation that everybody thought was dead and bringing it back to life. (Read the story about when Lazarus died in John chapter 11) Your time is coming but you have to let Adam rest for now.

What does it mean for Adam to rest? When God puts a man to rest, He does this in order for that man to settle down and begin to abide wholly in the Lord. He teaches them how to dwell securely in His presence. Men were created to be doers. Once they receive a task they work at it constantly. However, every man needs a place and time to rest. Adam was diligently working in Eden until God put Him to rest. If Adam did not rest, God would not have taken out his rib to put inside of Eve. When a man comes to his "resting-place" that is when he allows God to take out of him the qualities he needs to find in his wife. God desires to be every man's resting-place. It is in Him that men can find everything they need.

There will always come a time in a man's life when he will begin to search for his place of rest. Unfortunately, many men think that place can be found in a woman. There is a problem that arises when a woman tries to be that "place". She can end up consciously or subconsciously causing that man to take His focus off of the Lord as his resting-place. She becomes like a "Delilah" to him, giving him a false sense of security and peace of mind. This woman may think that she is only trying to guarantee herself a husband. In essence, she is trying to fulfill a role that was only meant for God. Women do many things to try and gain the attention of men so that the men may feel secure and relaxed with them. However, if these men have not yet learned to rest in the Lord, the women are out of God's order. *Women need to let the men rest.*

If we wake up children while they are resting, they will wake up cranky and they usually don't want to be bothered.

This is the same thing that can happen with the children of God. If we wake up our mates before it is time to be presented to them, we may just end up getting our feelings hurt. Perhaps a lack of rest may be the reason why some men do the things that hurt a lot of women. Maybe it is not so much that these men are "no good", they may just still be cranky and in need of rest. Many women were so quick to grab a mate that they didn't realize that he was still *half-asleep*. This is not how God intended to present us to our mates. Let's make sure that we are careful not to wake up God's children before their time.

We should want our mates to rest before God gives them to us. Why? First of all, someone who has learned to rest in the Lord's bosom is someone who has a personal relationship with the Lord. He will not be someone who has no clue as to how to talk to God and how to listen for His voice. David understood this when he wrote in Ps 37:7:

"Rest in the LORD, and wait patiently for him". (NKJV)

He knew that it was beneficial for man to rest in God. Later on in Psalm 37 he wrote:
"The steps of a good man are ordered by the Lord and He delights in his way. Though he fall, he shall not be utterly cast down; for the Lord upholds him with His hand." (NKJV)
David knew the Lord because David knew how to rest in Him. As a result, he learned to put his trust wholly in the Lord.

Even with blindfolds on I would quickly know whether I was in my own bed or someone else's because my bed is the one I have been consistently at rest in. I feel comfortable in it because I have come to be familiar with it. That is how God wants His children to rest in Him, feeling comfortable in His embrace.

Another reason why we should allow our potential mates to rest is because lack of rest can affect someone's vision. When I am really tired I don't see as clearly. Things become blurred in my sight. If our mates are to be the heads of our households, we should want their vision to be clear. How can one lead us without clear vision? A household will not be truly blessed unless the "head" can see the vision that God has for the house. Not getting enough rest can also affect what our mates hear from the Lord. God may be trying to give him direction but if he keeps drifting in and out of a "sleepy" state he will end up getting only a portion of the Word that God is sending to his house.

I may seem as though I am exaggerating this point; however, this is what is taking place in the marriages of many couples today. Many women have awakened their "Adam" before he was finished resting in the Lord. As a result, their households are suffering. These women begin to complain that their husbands aren't spiritual enough or that their husbands don't present themselves to be strong godly leaders of the household. How can they be if they are tired?

When someone gets a good rest, his mind, body, and spirit can operate effectively. We tend to think clearer after a good night's sleep.

Let Adam rest. It is a good thing to have a well-rested man who has learned to rest in his mind, body, and spirit. A man that feels "fatigued" in any one of these areas is someone you might have to drag around. We need someone who is wide awake whether we are stepping in the enemy's territory to tear down his kingdom or whether we are having a praise party in the presence of the Lord. Leave Adam alone to rest so that God can complete both of you. How can the Lord give us what our "Adam" needs if we don't allow him to rest?

Say this prayer with me right now:

My dear Lord, You are God all by Yourself and You don't need any tips on how to bless me. What You really need is for me to wait on You. Lord I will wait, from this moment on, with a willing and humble spirit. Help me to serve You and others with a spirit of excellence. The only way I can obtain a "Ruth" blessing is through diligently serving You and the "Naomi(s)" You send in my life. Help me to leave behind whatever I must depart from in order that I may serve as Ruth served. If ever there comes a time when my Naomi gives me good and godly counsel, help me to recognize that it is from You then help me to heed that counsel. If Your will for me is to have a mate one day, I pray that you teach me to be a wise shopper. Don't let me put in my heart what doesn't belong. Also, don't allow me to pass by what belongs to me. Make me recognizable to the mate You wish to present me to and I promise not to awaken him until he has fully learned to rest in You. I do all this in Your Holy name. Amen.

Finally…I Will

Throughout this book I have talked about being ready for a future mate, but what if God wishes for us to remain single for the rest of our lives? What if His desire is for us to remain married to Him alone? We can't hold our breath and expect our mates to arrive. What if those arms never come to hold us? Will we deprive ourselves of a blissful marriage with the Lord to wait for someone else?

I believe that we <u>all</u> should experience a blissful marriage. That marriage should be to our God. It is so imperative that we establish a love covenant with Christ and experience His true love for us. Don't make the mistake of neglecting His love for you while you wait for someone else to sweep you off your feet. God is so in love with His people. He wishes for us to wrap ourselves in His love. Even if there is a chance that we won't get married to a man one day, we all have an opportunity to experience the joys of a marriage. God will always be everything we need and more. He never changes. He doesn't leave His socks all over the floor. Instead, what He leaves are places of serenity and peace for us to pick up that surpass our understanding. You'll never have to remind Him to take out the trash. If we repent and confess our sins, He'll throw them out every time. He's not the kind of husband that constantly leaves the toilet seat up. Instead, what He leaves up are each one of our blessings to rain down on us at the appointed times. He can be the Husband that we need. We just have to be willing to give Him that chance.

If it is God's will for any of us to marry, that is also a wonderful thing. May the blessings of the Lord be upon the marriages of those who have waited on Him for their future mates. However, just as marriage is a gift from God, so is celibacy. If celibacy is your gift, don't despise it or feel as though God is short-changing you. He's got more in store for you than you could ever dream or imagine. I can hear someone saying *I just don't want to be lonely for the rest of my life*. Just because you are single or stand alone, does not mean that you have to be lonely. You can be lonely surrounded by a room full of people. It has happened to me. I have been lonely but not alone. I have had relationships where I would spend almost "24/7" with a person yet still feel a loneliness inside that could not be verbalized. Whenever I was asked what was wrong, I couldn't even begin to find the words within to explain myself. As a matter of fact, I had no idea why I was feeling so empty. Afterwards I realized that the emptiness was there because I had not let God fill my void, He taught me how to be alone yet not at all lonely inside. Loneliness is a feeling. Feelings can be controlled. You have the power to change how you feel. People feel lonely not necessarily because they are alone but because when that feeling first came their way they failed to change it. You change a "bad" feeling by exchanging it for a "good" feeling.

Whenever I start to feel periods of loneliness in my life, I immediately exchange it for a feeling that helps me not to feel that way. Notice I put that last sentence in the present tense. Loneliness does not just rear its ugly head one time in your life and then it's gone. It's liable to appear at any given time in your life. Just because it comes, doesn't mean it has to stay. You can combat loneliness in so many ways. Surround yourself by others in your church and fellowship with them. Pick up your favorite hobby. Practice a skill and consume yourself in the creativity God has blessed you with. Let God work on perfecting your ministry and ministry gifts. Most of all spend time with the One who is the Master at taking away the loneliness. The Lord will wrap you in His arms so tight that He'll make you forget you have not yet seen His blessed face. If you are constantly feeling lonely and sad it is because you failed to make an appointment with the Comforter. Like the comforter that you place on your bed at night, if you wrap up in Him, He'll take your mind off whatever has come to trouble your rest.

"Come unto me, all ye that labour and are heavy laden, and I will give you rest." **Matt 11:28** (KJV)

So, for all the sisters who are so busy searching for their "knights in shining armor" that they have not taken the time to fully tap into God's love, STOP. Wrap your arms around the One who longs to marry you, the Lord of hosts is His name.

We are "womb-men" simply because we have been formed out of men. The Lord is the only One who can make us a "good thing", whether for Himself alone or for our future mates as well. In Him is where we truly learn about love, joy, peace, and satisfaction. It is in those quiet mornings with Him that we will learn the art of communication. It is in those stormy nights that we develop trust. Bishop T.D. Jakes wrote in the Woman Thou Art Loosed edition Holy Bible "Gospel Pearls",[4] "God has a special anointing for the woman who is free to seek Him. Her prayer life should explode in miracles".

I pray that you have chosen to get closer to Jesus. He loves you. No matter how close you feel you are you can always get closer to Him. Reach out for the Lord and when

He takes your hand don't let His go. Caress Him and embrace Him. Love Him for He first loved you.

For the single women who know God has a mate for them, my sisters, you too need to be married to the Lord. It is during this season that He will "make" you for someone else. There is only one place He can make you, in His arms. Believe me, sometimes this season can get lonely, it might even seem desolate. Yet there is no other place I'd rather be during this time, but in the arms of Jesus. It is time for us all to tell the Lord *Finally...I will*. He is waiting for us to enter into a love affair that will certainly bring us beyond the veil of His presence. Before you say *I do*, make sure you tell Him *I will*.

I pray that this book has been a blessing to your spirit. Grace and peace be unto you and may God bless you during this season and every season that is to follow in your relationship with the Lover of your soul.

Lord, I thank you for the woman who longs to give her heart to You. I thank you for how You order her every step. She is exceedingly blessed to be loved by You. There is not an evening that You neglect to tuck her in the bed, pulling over her sheets of solace and peace. There is not a morning that passes by where You have failed to sprinkle the sunlight across her face. Teach her, oh Lord, how to give love back to You. Show her what it really means to be the wife of a living and loving God. Reel her heart into Your tender arms and embrace her with Your love. Only then can she experience fullness of joy. Only then can she truly become satisfied in this season. This I ask in Your precious name. Amen.

Nikki Simone

Bibliography

1. Terry Nance — Terry Nance, "God's Armorbearer II"
2. Bishop T.D. Jakes — Bishop T.D. Jakes, "The Lady, The Lover, and The Lord"
3. Dr. Ron Rannikar — Dr. Ron Ranniker, "Choosing God's Best"
4. Bishop T.D. Jakes — Bishop T.D. Jakes, "Gospel Pearls" from the Holy Bible, Woman Thou Art Loosed Edition

Nikki Simone

About the Author

Nikki Simone is a sure inspiration to single women of all ages. She is indeed an author to keep watching, a talented and anointed writer with a heart after God's own heart. She not only writes with an anointing, but walks in it as well. Since the day she accepted the Lord in her heart at eight years old, she has been in a relationship with Christ. In her journey through God's love she learned how to be the wife she always dreamed to become. She is free, yet focused; single, yet satisfactorily married to her Lord and Savior, Jesus Christ. In her debut book, *Before I Do... I Will,* she reveals to others the secrets of being a wife to God.

Nikki Simone speaks from the heart to the souls of single women, inclining and directing their hearts to embrace the blessedness of their season of singleness as they become enraptured by God's unfailing love. She now lives in New Jersey.

Printed in the United States
5221